PART ONE

One

November 14, 1997

At approximately 1:48 P.M., Deputy Darrin Zudel of the Genesee County Sheriff's Department (GCSD), while working district E-2 in the town of Genesee, Michigan, was dispatched to Fisherman's Park at the northeast corner of Bray and Carpenter Roads. The dispatcher said it was a possible DOA (dead on arrival).

When Zudel got to the park, he found three men and one woman, all in their early twenties. They were the ones who had called in the "911". It seemed that they had gone fishing in the park. On their way to the river, they had discovered a body.

"Stay back," Zudel told them.

Along with two EMTs who had just arrived on the scene, Zudel set out along the path the fishermen had been on only moments before when they made their discovery.

It didn't really look like much, sort of like a package all bundled up in a blanket. Zudel pulled the blanket down from the face and noted that the subject was a woman with blood around the head and also bruising to the face and eyes. He reached down, pulled the blanket aside from her right arm, and put his hand on her right wrist. The body was very, very cold. He was not surprised when he didn't feel any pulse.

Leaving the body with the two EMTs, Zudel went back to his car. By that time, Lieutenant Michael Becker of the Genessee County Sheriff's Department had arrived. Becker had been on uniformed duty when he heard Zudel being summoned and had raced to the scene as fast as he could.

Zudel took Becker back along the trail; Zudel showed him the body. From Becker's preliminary examination, it was clear the woman had been murdered. It was time to bring in a specialist.

Kevin Shanlian was in his office at the Genesee County Sheriff's Department when he, too, heard Central Communication dispatch Zudel's unit to the fishing site located at Bray and Carpenter Roads.

While the park was technically in the township of Genesee, it was located right next to Flint. Flint, Michigan, has one of the highest per capita murder rates in the country. Murders, though, didn't just stop at the city line. They leached over. Unfortunately, homicides were anything but rare in Genesee. Commonplace was a more apt description.

Immediately a question of jurisdiction came up. While the park was in Genesee Township, the township was within the county of the same name. Therefore, who had jurisdiction? Actually, the answer was both, but the township's police force had two detectives on leave and was understaffed. As a result, they made the practical decision to shift responsibility to the sheriff.

The next call Shanlian heard was from his lieutenant, Michael Becker, summoning him to the scene. The body dump job would be his case. Shanlian reached into his desk.

When he had first started as a rookie, he probably had eight guns on him and a knife in his boot. But the more experience he got, the more he realized how much you used your head on the job. He got to putting the gun in a drawer or in a glove compartment, having to remind himself to take it out when he went into the field.

Now he reached into his desk and took out his 45mm Sig Sauer automatic and snapped it in place in the shoulder holster under his jacket. It was a lot of firepower, but Flint was a high crime area and cops were always one step behind the bad guys when it came to firepower.

He drove quickly to the scene. By the time he got there, the temperature had risen to all of thirty-three degrees, a veritable heat wave in the late Michigan fall.

"She's along that path there," Lieutenant Becker told Shanlian, pointing behind him.

Becker was busy answering half a dozen questions from support personnel. Alone, Shanlian walked along the path and into the park.

The warmer air had mixed with the colder ground producing a fog that hung low to the earth, swirling around the body of the woman, who looked so warm and comfy wrapped in the flowered blanket that had become her death shroud.

Who was she? How had she gotten there?

Shanlian, a veteran detective at thirty-five, spotted Deputy Zudel, the cop who had first called the homicide in.

"Have the fishermen who discovered the body transported to headquarters, where we'll take their statements. Then go check the trash containers around here and the roadway west of here," Shanlian requested. "Let's see if we can find any evidence that might help us."

Turning to another cop, Officer Pilon, Shanlian asked him to check the trash containers and roadways east of the murder scene. Then he asked Detective Dwayne Cherry to work the death scene as a liaison between the investigating detectives and the Michigan State Police Crime Laboratory out of Bridgeport, Michigan. The latter had been summoned to collect physical evidence at the death scene. It was specifically labeled "death scene," as opposed to "crime scene," because while the body had been discovered there, they didn't know yet where she had been murdered.

He sent a fourth officer back to headquarters to retrieve footwear and a tire impression collection kit. Maybe they'd get lucky and find that the killer or killers had left footprints around the body.

Cops hated body dump jobs. It was like someone just dropped the damn corpse from a plane and then it was the cop's turn to figure out who it was and how it got there. It was a good thing Shanlian had a sense of humor. Otherwise, the body dumps he'd investigated over his sixteen years as a cop would have gotten to him. There were so many, he couldn't count them up even if he had four sets of hands and feet.

Trying to deduce how the killer or killers had dumped the body, Shanlian immediately noted its location in a clearing and the two paths that cut through. Shanlian saw a narrow, maybe two-inch path of what appeared to be burned leaves leading from the parking lot, through the woods, stopping at the asphalt footpath. He went over to view the body and immediately smelled the gasoline on her. He looked back at the burned leaves. Shanlian figured they were trying to burn the body by setting a fuse made out of leaves.

If the flames had actually hit the body, they

would have consumed it, throwing the identification process into a more difficult mode than it already was in. The problem for the killer or killers was that the flame went out when the fire hit the asphalt path. This left the body intact, along with hopes of a quick identification.

The cop came back to the death scene with the vehicle impression kit. Assisted by his partner, Chuck Melki, Shanlian made plaster impressions of an unknown vehicle tire impression in the parking lot. The two detectives photographed all the witnesses' and officers' shoe prints that had entered the crime scene. Shanlian also shot all the vehicle tires that had entered the adjacent parking lot. These photographs would later serve to eliminate police and civilian personnel as offering no significance to the commission of the crime.

Up to that point, the victim had remained where she was, no more than an insignificant part of the landscape. Now she became an active participant in her own murder investigation.

Taking care to pull on rubber gloves, so as not to "infect" the evidence, Shanlian carefully pulled the blanket down to examine her.

Her face was bloody and bruised. Over her left eye in particular, extending back to her ear and down to her cheek, was one reddish and bluish bruise, like a giant discolored birthmark. There were also multiple lacerations. The eye had received so much trauma, it appeared to have swelled shut as a result.

Around her neck was a necklace with a small cocaine spoon attached. Now that was interesting. Maybe this was a drug-related murder. Continuing his examination, Shanlian saw that the victim was wrapped in a bedspread, which was black in color with a green and pink flower design imprinted on it.

The woman wore black Chic brand pants pulled down and around her left ankle. Her socks were black in color. She wore only one left shoe, black Guess brand. The victim's red underpants had been pulled down, wrapped around her left thigh near the vagina. They had certainly been pulled down for a reason; it was too early in the investigation to tell why.

Her stomach had two small brownish and blackish wounds, about three inches in diameter. Farther down, there was a small bruise on her right thigh, then another circular wound up near the vagina. Finally, on the inner side of the right ankle, Shanlian discovered a fifth wound, again about three inches in diameter, brownish and blackish in color.

The victim was wearing a maroon-colored, short-sleeved polo shirt with SOUTH BOULEVARD STATION emblazoned over the left breast. Neither shirt nor bra appeared to have been disturbed. If she'd been raped, the killer had not touched her breasts.

On her arms, right on top of the right biceps,

was what appeared to be a burn mark. Had the woman been tortured before she died? Underneath the arm, in the arm joint, was a second burn mark, though this appeared more like a brownish or blackish wound. There was frayed skin and discoloration around her right wrist consistent with a ligature wound. That is, someone had bound her wrist before she died.

Shanlian picked up her right hand and noticed a gold-colored ring with a large sapphire on her ring finger. Underneath her fingernail was blood and something else. Forensics would take those scrapings; hopefully, they'd lead to something.

Shanlian didn't see any injuries on her left arm, though her left fingernails had blood underneath them. Her left thumbnail and part of the tip of the thumb had a large cut on it. This was consistent with defensive wounds. But the cut appeared to have teeth marks on it. Had someone bitten her to get her to stop defending herself?

As with the right wrist, the left had a ligature wound, too. Unless forensics could offer another explanation, that meant she had been bound before she died.

"Let's turn her," Shanlian said.

He and Melki reached down and turned her onto her stomach.

There was no clue under her, no weapon, no anything except blanket and earth. They pulled up her shirt to examine her back.

Shanlian saw that it was a speckled shade of red indicating lividity; that is, a settling of the blood into that region. Since lividity had already set in, and rigor mortis, the stiffness that immediately accompanies death, had receded, it was safe to assume that she had been dead for over thirty hours. Unless, of course, someone had thrown her into a freezer to slow the whole "decomp" process down, which would completely foul things up.

Shanlian surmised that the victim's attire was consistent with that of a waitress, someone who probably worked for a business called South Boulevard Station. If the killer was trying to make sure that identification was difficult, he never should have left the shirt on. Then again, he probably figured quite rightly that if the body burned, there would be no shirt left.

Searching through her pockets, Shanlian came up empty. No identification whatsoever. She also had no purse, no backpack, no nothing. Considering that she still had her ring on, they could eliminate robbery as a motive.

Today was Friday, casual day, and Shanlian had dressed in an open-necked sport shirt with jeans. When he had gotten the call, he had thrown on his sweater and overcoat and had raced to the scene. Now, he pulled his overcoat tighter around himself, but it did nothing to keep the chill out. Maybe he was getting too old for this work. Or maybe it was just the viciousness of the murder he was trying to keep out.

Shanlian stopped his musings. That was a luxury for another time. He reached inside his jacket to his belt, reminding himself that he had brought his gun.

He pulled out his cell phone; he always carried it with him now. It was de rigueur police equipment, a Nextel phone, broadcasting over digital lines so slaphappy hackers couldn't listen in on the scrambled channels like they did on scanners. Most surveillance these days was done the same way and for the same reasons.

His digital call was to the county's on-duty medical examiner, Dr. Wilys Mueller. He gave him permission to move the body. When the techies and police photographer were finished, the body would be transported to the county morgue. He also called Sergeant Ives Potrafka of his department and requested he come to the crime scene as soon as possible. Then it was a quick call to the on-duty county prosecutor, David Newblatt, who authorized the autopsy for the following morning at 11:00.

Next up was a check of missing person reports. Shanlian called the Flint Police and Central Dispatch and requested a search of all recent missing W/F reports that matched the victim's description.

That brought negative results quickly: he could find no one missing who fit the dead woman's description. Shanlian responded with a Statewide Administrative message, what used to be known as an All Points Bulletin (APB), requesting information on any recent missing person reports. Trying to match those to the victim also proved a negative result.

Sometimes, bad guys are captured on videotape before they commit the murder. There was one case in Tampa, Florida, where a serial killer named Sam Smithers walked into a convenience store with his victim, bought some stuff, and less than a half hour later killed her. The tape allowed the prosecutors to put him together with the victim before the murder took place. Shanlian requested that detectives retrieve any video surveillance from area gas stations.

A few minutes later, Sergeant Ives Potrafka of the sheriff's office arrived on the scene to assist Shanlian.

"Ives, I want you to maintain the crime scene in order to free up other detectives for further investigation."

It was a boring but important job; Potrafka had to maintain the integrity of the scene, not allow anyone to contaminate it and make sure that any evidence gathered by the Michigan Police Crime Lab found its way to Shanlian immediately. Most importantly, Potrafka would be in charge of making sure the body got transported to the morgue after the crime scene was completely processed.

Looking down at the victim's T-shirt, Shanlian knew he didn't have to be a Ph.D. to figure out what was next. He asked a female deputy to call all the local area codes and see if she could locate a restaurant called South Boulevard Station. She came back a few minutes later with the answer. There was a restaurant by that name in Auburn Hills.

Auburn hills. That was only an hour's drive south. Shanlian hypothesized that maybe she was killed down there and dumped in his bailiwick. He wouldn't know for sure until he went down there.

Two

Seated beside Shanlian's desk at headquarters was Bobby Lee Locke. Twenty-three years old, he worked for a local cable company. Like most people, he had never been involved with violence, let alone murder. That all changed when he and his friends Del Crane, Alex Sexton and Dee Ryan had taken time off from work to go ice fishing at a county park set beside the Flint River in Flint, Michigan.

They got there a little before 1:00 P.M., he told Shanlian. As they got out of their van, their breath plumed out like smoke. The temperature was hovering just above freezing. The park was beautiful in the spring, summer and early fall. But by late fall, it was a dead place. Brown leaves that had not been covered by the white stuff lay lifeless on the snow-encrusted ground. Their boots crunched beneath them. They trekked east into the park, going toward the river, which was stocked with that delicious fish that would make an excellent dinner.

The pathway ran east from the parking lot, eventually terminating at the river. Trees bordered the trail, their naked branches hibernating against the coming winter. Across from them, running in the opposite direction, was a bicycle path, deserted and forlorn in the late-fall sun.

There was a slight wind. It made them pull their collars up and huddle down inside their coats. Over their shoulders they carried their poles, the party looking like some late-twentieth-century version of Huck Finn, Tom Sawyer and Becky Thatcher out for a little fishing and partying. And just like Mark Twain's heroes, they ran into trouble.

Fifty feet in front of them was something wrapped up in a blanket. They stopped. Del thought it looked like a body. Dee thought it was a deer or a dog. They continued hiking but stopped when they got to it.

Bobby kicked out and struck it with his foot. His face turned a ghostly pallor when he realized he had kicked someone's leg. They all freaked and ran back to the van. When they got there, they discussed what to do. Bobby and Del decided to go back and check to make sure they weren't crazy.

They weren't. They wound up gazing down at a body. They ran back, found a phone, and dialed 911.

"And that's all I know," Bobby concluded.

That all jibed with what Shanlian knew.

"Thanks for your statement," Shanlian said. "If we need you, we'll call you."

He watched as the dazed young man wound his way through the room, tightly packed with desks and chairs and detectives on phones, and disappeared down the stairs at the far end.

"Kevin."

Shanlian looked up. It was Melki. While Shanlian had been conducting the interview with Locke, Melki had called the restaurant South Boulevard Station in Auburn Hills. He discovered that a waitress named Nancy Billiter had not shown up for work the previous night. She was usually a punctual person, so the restaurant manager was worried.

The manager supplied a description of Nancy Billiter. It matched that of the "Jane Doe" discovered in the park in Flint.

Shanlian and Melki felt a bit cocky. Who could blame them? They'd just beaten the odds. It wasn't very often you could establish the identity in a body dump case with a few phone calls, but it looked like they had. But as quickly as he'd gone up, Shanlian came down.

He knew that the body was only the beginning. Its discovery was just the end of a long set of circumstances that led to murder. Where it really got interesting was the discovery of the killer and, hopefully, the motive. Motive isn't necessary to convict, but it sure helps the jury convict the bad guy if they can understand why the crime was committed.

There was, of course, no guarantee there would be a trial. Or, an accused. District attorneys don't like to talk about it, lest the voting populace kicks them out of office, but the fact is that every day in America, the perfect crime is committed. Many killers are never identified and are free to kill again.

Shanlian and his partner, Melki, knew all this. No cop likes to admit that a bad guy can outwit him or her and get away with murder, but they all know it happens. Shanlian just hoped that this wouldn't be one of those times.

Shanlian and Melki bundled into their topcoats. They got into their unmarked Ford Taurus and headed south on Interstate 75. Their destination was the Detroit suburb of Auburn Hills. Shanlian gazed out into the night that had seemed to fall so fast in late afternoon.

He wasn't thinking that someplace out there in the towns where lights were just coming on to illuminate the encroaching darkness there was a bullet with his name on it. Sure, once in a while there was that mortal chance of encountering a murderer who was packing and who decided he didn't want to be taken in to face a trial and a life sentence, who pulls that weapon and fires. Like anytime he went into the field, Shanlian just hoped that no one would be firing any weapons.

No, what he was really concerned about, what he was really thinking about, was the case itself.

The biggest danger to a homicide cop was that the job would seep through that barrier he'd built up in his brain between his professional and personal life. What was to be feared on a regular basis was not the murderer's bullets but the grief of the loved ones the victim left behind; it was not the knife of the murderer but the rage behind the blade, the anger that propelled the crime and caused a human being to abandon all civilized behavior and instead resort to deadly force.

Grief, rage, anger. It was only so long, only so many years of visiting crime scenes, before the brain went toxic from it all.

Kevin Shanlian and Chuck Melki got to the Auburn Hills Police Department at 6:50 P.M. They had called earlier to say they were coming down and working a murder case. Since it was still not clear who would have venue in the case—because no one yet knew where the suspected victim Nancy Billiter had died—Detective Scott Edwards of the Auburn Hills Police Department had been assigned to the case.

"Look, I have a contact at South Boulevard Station," he told Shanlian and Melki. "I already called over there."

Edwards had gone ahead and questioned the people over at the restaurant and found out Billiter's last-known address and her physical description.

"She matches the victim," he said simply.

He had also gotten a list of her relatives.

"Okay, let's go over to the restaurant," said Shanlian. "We still need a positive ID."

They drove through the wind and cold, through the air filled with moisture coming off Lake Michigan. The car's heater wasn't the greatest in the world; the cold air seemed to go right through them, chilling their bones. But when they got to South Boulevard Station a few minutes later, they found it warm and comfortable inside.

Edwards flashed the tin and asked the bartender where the manager was. The bartender motioned to a back office, where they found Eddie Grant.

"Yes, I'm the manager. How can I help you?" said Grant.

"You have an employee named Nancy Billiter," asked Edwards.

"Yes. She's been out the last two nights."

"What does she look like?"

"Well, she's about forty-five, about five three, one hundred thirty pounds or so."

"Hair and eyes?"

"Sort of reddish blond and blue eyes. Hey, you the cops who called?"

None of the cops answered yet. They needed more.

"What about her work uniform? Could you describe it, please?" Shanlian asked easily.

"Uh, it's a pullover shirt that comes in three colors—green, tan or burgundy."

"Pants?"

"Black jeans."

"And the last time you saw her?" said Melki.

According to Grant, Billiter had volunteered to come into work on her day off, Wednesday, but she did not show up. He called her house several times to see what was going on but got no response. When he thought about it, Grant realized he actually hadn't seen her since she left work on Tuesday night. Shanlian asked if he had her time card handy. Grant quickly came up with it and handed it over.

Gazing at the machine-printed notations, Shanlian saw that Billiter had punched out of work on Tuesday, November 11, at 9:09 P.M., after working the second shift.

"Actually, the time clock is off by an hour," Grant added, "so Nancy actually worked until nine after ten."

Shanlian knew that sometime after that and before this afternoon, someone killed her. The detective reached inside the breast pocket of his sport jacket and came out with a picture.

"Mr. Grant, that's a death scene photograph of a victim in our county we are trying to iden-tify."

He handed it over.

"Would you look at it, please?"

Grant took a deep breath and held it in his hands like some valuable relic. He gazed at the picture of the bloody face wrapped up in the flowered blanket and then looked up. He had a confused, shocked expression on his face.

"That's Nancy," he said simply.

"Nancy Billiter?" Shanlian asked.

"Yes."

Had anyone been calling and asking for her recently? Shanlian wondered.

"Nancy's friend, Carol, had called a little while ago. She said she hadn't seen Nancy since Tuesday and she was worried," Grant replied.

"You have Carol's address?"

"Yeah."

He looked in a filing cabinet and came out with Billiter's file, which had her phone number and her address. She had lived only a few miles from the restaurant. He copied it onto a sheet of white paper that he gave to Shanlian.

"She lived with her mother. Look, I should also tell you," Grant said reluctantly, "that Nancy was using cocaine. She was a good waitress and everything, but she had a problem with the drug."

"Anyone else here who Nancy knew or was close with?"

"Yeah, she was friends with Kip Selbach, one of the waiters. I'll get him for you."

A few minutes later, Grant came back with Selbach, a tall, good-looking man in his early thirties. He said that he'd known Billiter for a few years and they'd become friends. Shanlian showed him the crime scene photograph and Selbach identified Billiter immediately.

Shanlian asked him what was she wearing the

last time he saw her. He was trying to determine if she had time to go home and change. Or, did the murder take place before she got home?

Selbach was certain that the last time he saw her, Billiter was wearing her burgundy work shirt, black jeans, jeans jacket and black tennis shoes. That was an exact match to the clothing the "Jane Doe" had been found in.

"Nancy had waited at the restaurant for about an hour after punching out on Tuesday. Four of the regulars had offered her a ride home, but she turned them all down."

"Who drove her then?" chimed in Edwards.

"I don't know."

"What time did she finally leave?" asked Edwards again.

"Around eleven P.M."

They had just cut two hours off the time frame, from 9:00 to 11:00 P.M. Two hours less to figure out what had happened before Nancy Billiter died. But they needed to get even more specific.

Shanlian wondered if there was anyone else she was friendly with, and Selbach recalled she was friendly with Yvonne Craig, the receptionist. A few minutes later, Grant brought in a petite blonde with a knockout figure.

"I only knew Nancy a couple of months. I met her here at work," said Yvonne somewhat defensively.

"She used cocaine?" Shanlian asked.

"Yeah, I guess; yeah, she had a cocaine problem."

"When'd you see her last?"

"Around ten o'clock on Tuesday, when Bill Bernhard drove her home." Bernhard was a regular at the restaurant. "I loaned him my car to drive her home. He came back around eleven and gave me the keys and then Bill stayed until closing time."

Craig figured closing time for about one o'clock. She didn't know Bernhard well, only from the restaurant. She had no idea where he lived.

"What was Mr. Bernhard like when he came back?" Shanlian asked.

"Like how?"

"Was he upset? Were his clothes disheveled?"

"No. No. He was real calm."

"Was there anything out of place in your car? Anything that looked upset?"

Translation: Any blood or weapons in the car? How about a dead body?

"No. It was the same as when I gave him the keys."

"How was Nancy acting in the last week?" Shanlian asked. "Was everything all right with her?"

"Well, Nancy was upset last week because her roommate, Carol, was accusing her of stealing from her. Nancy had told Carol that someone had broken into her house, but Carol was suspicious. She didn't believe that."

Yvonne wasn't sure what Carol's last name was, but she thought it might be "Giles." She thought that Carol lived on Orchard Lake Road in Bloomfield but couldn't be sure.

Edwards told the Flint cops that West Bloomfield was the next town over. He went out to the pay phone and called Information, trying to get an address for Bill Bernhard. But Bernhard wasn't listed with Information and Edwards didn't want to take the time right then to check with motor vehicles. Besides, it didn't sound like Bernhard had had anything to do with the murder.

On his second call to Information, Edwards was able to locate an address for a Carol Giles. She lived on Walnut Lake Road in West Bloomfield Township.

At 9:00 P.M., the cops left the restaurant. The Slocum address Grant had given them, where Nancy Billiter lived with her mother, was only a few blocks from the restaurant. They pulled up to the modest house at 9:07 P.M. The name on the curbside mailbox was BURKE. Shanlian figured that must be the mother's name. Walking up the tree-lined driveway, they felt the chill wind picking up.

It was Phyllis Burke, Nancy Billiter's sixty-four-year-old mother, who answered the doorbell. She opened the door and looked at three tall, burly-looking men in overcoats.

Edwards flashed the tin. He explained that they were police officers investigating a crime and that her daughter might be involved. The three men stepped inside; Burke had enough presence of mind to close the door behind them. Immediately, Shanlian asked her if she had a photograph of Nancy Billiter. His tone was gentle, considering the urgency of the circumstances.

Not saying a word, with a creeping dread in her heart, Phyllis Burke went into the living room and came back with a framed snapshot of a smiling middle-aged woman. Shanlian pulled the picture from his pocket and compared them.

The woman was the same in both photographs.

"I'm sorry to have to tell you, but Nancy has been murdered."

Burke began sobbing, great heaves of grief. She called her two daughters, Susan Garrison and Karen Clason, and told them, "The police are here. They say Nancy has been murdered." The girls said they'd be right there.

"Mrs. Burke, when was the last time you saw your daughter?" Edwards asked.

"Not for over a week," she replied, wiping tears from her face.

They had had a big argument and she had asked her daughter to leave. Shanlian figured it must have been one hell of an argument.

"When was that?" Melki asked.

"Early October, I think it was the ninth. Even

though Nancy was the legal guardian, I been taking care of my great-grandson since."

Just then, the front door opened and an attractive woman walked in.

"Oh, Mom," she said, and ran to her mother and put her arms around her. They hugged for a long, interminable moment, the cops shuffling their feet awkwardly, until they broke the embrace and the woman introduced herself.

"I'm Karen Clason, Nancy's sister."

Shanlian sized her up as a woman in her late thirties or early forties. A moment later, the door opened and another woman ran in, looking a lot like the other two in the room. She, too, embraced Burke and then introduced herself as Susan Garrison, Nancy's other sister.

Shanlian suggested that while Melki and Edwards talk to Mrs. Burke, the sisters and he go into another room to talk. The two sisters followed him into a bedroom, where they began to talk about their sister.

Nancy Billiter's partner, the one she lived with day and night, thought about, and worked her ass off for, was cocaine.

Sober, Nancy could function at work, but as soon as she was off, she craved that hit that made her forget her troubles and put her into another, safer, warmer place.

Susan Garrison was aware that her older sister Nancy Billiter had a problem with drugs, but Billiter had reassured her that that was in the past. Garrison had no reason to doubt her.

Nancy and her siblings, Susan, Karen and Doug, had grown up as part of a close-knit family in the middle-class Detroit suburb of Auburn Hills. Headquarters for the Chrysler Corporation, the town was a combination of upper- and middle-class families. The former were the executives, the latter the workers, either in the auto plant or the various businesses that fed off the business of building cars.

Growing up, the Burke children were happy. Then, when Nancy was eight years old, their father was killed in a car accident. At twenty-six, Phyllis Burke was left a widow with five kids. She didn't work.

Garrison recalled that they lived off SSI and from people helping out. The siblings became very self-sufficient in helping out their mother. They became even closer knit.

Perhaps because of the trauma involved, Susan, who was six years old when her father died, didn't remember that time of life. What she did remember was sharing a room with Nancy.

Susan and Nancy were into Barbie dolls. They shared the same clothes. It was the 1960s and they listened to the same music—the Beatles, Kinks, and Stones. Later on, when they hit their teens, if Nancy had a boyfriend, she'd introduce Susan and they would double-date.

The two-year age difference meant they were in the same high school at the same time. Nancy did nothing to distinguish herself there; she was just an average student who was into boys. But she had aspirations of being a nurse, and upon her graduation from high school, she began looking into the health profession. Life, though, threw her a curve.

Nancy got pregnant out of wedlock and had a baby she named Stacy. She decided to raise Stacy on her own and support her herself.

Nancy became a waitress. She was a personable, good worker and had no trouble finding jobs. For the next twenty years, she supported herself and her child with eight- to twelve-hour shifts. She was on her feet so much, it wasn't uncommon for her to come home with swollen legs. But she kept going—she had to. Her kid was relying on her, and nothing was more important to Nancy than her family.

In those years, the only real means of self-expression she had was sports. She was a great softball player. It was after high school that she got into sports, particularly softball. Nancy played shortstop and first base. She batted right-handed.

In between double plays, Nancy tried marriage. She was in her early thirties when she married Jimmy Ryan. She was quite a bit older than Jimmy, Susan recalled, and because of that and other reasons, it didn't work out.

After only a few months together, they separated and divorced.

Like most detectives, Shanlian knew that the homicide victim usually knows her killer; that is, it is usually a friend or family member who commits the crime. That was an angle he needed to pursue.

He wanted to know if when she was married to Jimmy Ryan, there was any history of domestic violence. Both women answered no. They insisted he couldn't be involved because the marriage took place ten years before; they didn't even know if Ryan was still local. That didn't let Ryan out, necessarily, but it did make him a remote suspect.

Garrison related how her niece Stacy, Nancy's daughter, eventually grew up and met a guy in Michigan, then moved with him to Georgia "and got herself in trouble there," Susan continued. "Nancy got custody of the baby."

By that time, Nancy had made an arrangement with her mother.

"The baby lived with Nancy and my mother."

Nancy had a grandchild to help support. But by that time, the 1990s, the pressure of a hard-scrabble existence had gotten to Nancy and she had taken up with cocaine. As Nancy moved from one high to another, she also changed jobs, until she wound up as a waitress at South Boulevard Station. Susan Garrison and her mom went there all the time.

They would have dinner and sit drinking coffee afterward for hours, until they floated out of there. The restaurant had a very comfortable atmosphere. Everyone was very friendly. When Nancy's grandson was about eight, Susan and her mom would occasionally take the boy to the restaurant for dinner during Nancy's shift.

Nancy doted on her grandchild and loved him more than anything else in the world. In fact, the only other man she loved as much was probably Jessie Giles.

What a wonderful guy Jessie was, how good to everyone. When he died, Nancy knew she would miss him. But who Giles was wasn't important right then. Shanlian needed to get her back on track. He asked them when was the last time they saw their sister.

The two women looked at each other and Karen replied not for about a week. Susan, a divorcée with three kids, said that sounded about right. Shanlian asked if they knew who supplied her with coke.

"I think it's a guy named Ben Drier," Karen Clason replied.

"You know how to spell his name?" asked Shanlian, taking notes.

"No. But I think he's about forty. That's what Nancy said," Clason continued.

Neither woman knew anything about Drier. Taking another tact, the detective wondered if anything had happened recently to upset Nancy. Turned out that Nancy was upset. Or actually, her roommate Carol was.

Carol's VCR had been stolen. She thought Nancy had stolen it. That was interesting, but Shanlian was having a problem.

"There's one thing I'm confused about," Shanlian said. "Nancy was living here with your mother, but she had a roommate named Carol?"

"Oh, that," Garrison answered. "Nancy really wasn't living there, just staying there with Carol to help her get through her grief."

"Grief?"

"Nancy was just helping Carol out with her house and kids and stuff. Carol's husband Jessie died a few months ago and she really needed the help."

"So she really lived here?"

Nancy and her mom had had an argument, but she still lived at home.

That was the second time the argument was mentioned. Shanlian had to wonder what kind of argument was so severe Nancy would have been forced to leave.

Could her mom have had an ax to grind? Phyllis Burke didn't look like a murderer, but then again, most murderers don't.

The sisters explained that while Nancy and their mom had argued they had pretty much patched things up. Nancy was just about to leave Carol's and move back in.

"Okay, would one of you please come down to identify Nancy? Perhaps tomorrow?"

Clason volunteered. Shanlian gave her the

morgue's address. The cops left Phyllis Burke's house at 9:45 P.M. The detectives had one more stop before calling it a night.

Three

Back in Genesee County, the body of Nancy Billiter was still lying where it was first found.

It had lain on the cold, hard ground since it was dumped. Because rigor mortis was gone by the time the body was discovered, the cops knew she had been there since long before dawn. Now, finally, the investigators had finished their death work and the body was ready to be removed.

Sergeant Ives Potrafka had done as Shanlian requested. He had preserved the integrity of the crime scene, making sure it wasn't contaminated.

At approximately 9:39 P.M., C&M Ambulance personnel carried a stretcher/gurney into the park and put it down next to the body. Gently they transferred it onto the stretcher, then lifted and carried it back out to the lot. When they hit the gravel, they let the legs of the gurney come down and they wheeled it over to their ambulance, where they picked it up and shoved it in.

Sergeant Potrafka followed the body to Hur-

ley Medical Center. They arrived there at 9:55
P.M.

Under the direction of Dr. Grant Williams,
the medical examiner, the body was tagged and
placed into the hospital's morgue by registered
nurse Roger Gilmore. The autopsy would take
place tomorrow morning.

Satisfied that his charge was in safe hands,
Potrafka was able to go home and get some
sleep. It had been a very long day, he thought,
as he drove by the park.

The cops were still there.

Deputy Zudel had been instructed to stand
by at the crime scene until the Michigan State
lab techs completed clearing their equipment.
After that, it would be his job to remove the
yellow crime scene tape.

And after that, it would be like nothing had
happened.

As Edwards tooled the car through the dark,
snow covered streets of West Bloomfield Township, Shanlian pulled the crime scene photograph out of his pocket and examined it again.

Nothing had changed.

Nancy Billiter was still dead. Her face was
beaten in, dried blood in a gash across her
nose; the left side of her head and temple
showed a discolored shade of red; she wore the
burgundy T-shirt with the sporty SOUTH BOULE-
VARD STATION logo across the upper left breast.

"We're almost there," said Edwards.

Shanlian stuffed the picture back in his pocket.

"West Bloomfield Township police headquarters are in there," said Edwards, pointing out a sprawling, low-lying gray building.

They passed the police station and not more than ten seconds later, he pulled over to the curb on the right. Shanlian looked out at a small suburban house recessed from the curb about two hundred feet back, surrounded by oak trees. The mailbox had the address on it and the name GILES.

According to the people they'd interviewed so far, Carol Giles was Nancy's temporary roommate. Or was it the other way around? Whatever. Maybe Giles knew something that could help them track down Billiter's killer.

Edwards pulled the car up onto the driveway. Everything was dark. There was no driveway sensor light to light up the flagstone pathway that led up to the front door.

They tried peering inside the living room windows, but the inside drapes were drawn. They could see nothing, not even the outline of lights around the fabric. Maybe everyone was sleeping. They knocked on the door and tried the doorbell, but no one answered. If anyone was inside, they were certainly sound sleepers.

The next step was calling, but they didn't have the number.

Edwards went to the next-door neighbor,

flashed the tin again, and asked the man who answered the door if he had Giles's number. The guy came back with it a minute later. Back in the car, Shanlian tried the number on his cell phone. No answer. Just as he pressed a button to disconnect, the cops saw headlights turning into the Giles house.

Slowly a Mercury Sable pulled into the driveway and stopped. The headlights dimmed to nothing. Silence. The car door opened and a long leg came out, following by a body wrapped up in a winter coat. It was a woman. She walked to the front door, put a key in the lock, and disappeared inside. They had a reasonable certainty it was Carol Giles.

"Let's set up a surveillance," Shanlian suggested.

They couldn't very well do so without alienating the local cops; they were now operating in West Bloomfield Township. Edwards called the local cops down the block and explained to the desk sergeant what was going on. Minutes later, a marked unit that the sergeant dispatched pulled up to the curb. Edwards and Melki filled the uniforms in on the case and asked them to stay at the curb and provide any necessary assistance.

"Look!" Shanlian interrupted.

The woman had come out of the house and was getting in her car.

"Let's go," Shanlian ordered.

Shanlian got behind the wheel, and Edwards

and Melki tumbled in. Shanlian raced the car up the driveway. The woman put her car in gear and looked back. Squealing, the brakes bit and the cop car blocked the Sable from getting out. Startled, the beautiful, bespectacled twenty-something woman got out of her car. Edwards identified himself, Shanlian and Melki.

"Are you Carol Giles?" asked Edwards.

She nodded. Shanlian asked her when she had last seen her roommate Nancy Billiter.

"Uh, on Tuesday," Carol replied.

That would be Tuesday, November 11. Shanlian remembered that Nancy Billiter had been driven back to Giles's home at 11:00 P.M. on November 11. On a hunch, he decided to try something.

"We have witnesses that saw Nancy Billiter here on Wednesday, November twelfth."

It was a white lie, because Billiter could have left immediately on November 11 and gone someplace else. But Shanlian was betting that after a night on her feet, she had crashed without going anywhere. The idea was to narrow the time frame down, closer and closer to the time of the murder.

Do that and you move closer and closer to the murderer.

Carol Giles said she had seen Nancy Billiter on Wednesday, but that she left about 1:30 in the morning on Thursday and hadn't seen her since. Shanlian was following his feelings and his gut told him that something about the woman just didn't sit right.

If Billiter was a heavy drug user, as witnesses had said, wouldn't this woman Giles know about it? What kind of person lets a heavy drug user into her home?

"Are you carrying any drugs or weapons?" Shanlian asked suddenly.

Carol Giles could have easily answered no and walked away. If she did, there was nothing Shanlian could do. She wasn't under arrest. And if she wasn't under arrest, they had no constitutional right to search her. But cops know how to use intimidation to get what they want, and Shanlian had made his question sound very menacing, like "If you lie to me, I'm gonna search you."

"I have some drugs," Giles confessed.

Carol Giles pulled a small plastic Baggie with white powder in it from her overcoat pocket. Handing it over, she explained that it was crack.

"Would you empty your pockets for me?" Shanlian requested.

By voluntarily turning over the drugs, Giles had made herself a suspected felon. That made it constitutionally acceptable for Giles to be searched, by force if necessary. On the other hand, she hadn't yet been advised of her rights, so anything she said could not be used in court against her.

Carol Giles went over to her car. She emptied her right coat pocket. Out came a small electronic scale, the kind that could be used by a dealer to weigh dope. When she reached in her left, out came two syringes still in their protective plastic wrapping. Shanlian had to wonder if she was mainlining.

"I've also got a gun in the car," she added.

"Handgun?" Shanlian asked.

Giles nodded.

Shanlian didn't search the car. He wasn't sure of his constitutional grounds on that one. Instead, he asked if they could go in the house and Giles said sure.

Inside, they put the cocaine, the scale and the syringes on a coffee table next to a bong that was already there. Shanlian thought for a minute. If he arrested her on a drug beef, she might clam up. She had been cooperative for some unknown reason. Better to keep her cool.

"Mrs. Giles, you're not under arrest. Our department has no interest in the cocaine or handgun in your possession at this point. Do you own this house?"

"No, I'm a renter," she replied. "But my name is on the lease."

Shanlian looked around. It was plainly furnished with sofa, chairs, dining room set, a little bit in disarray with children's toys scattered about.

"Is anyone at home besides you?"

"No."

"And is the car outside yours?"

"Yes."

"Are you currently under the influence of any drugs or alcohol?" Shanlian asked.

If she was, that stopped his next request. A person under the influence does not have the ability to agree to a search that would be constitutionally acceptable.

"No," she replied.

Good, he thought.

"We'd like to search your residence and your vehicle," Shanlian asked. "For evidence of the homicide of Nancy Billiter," he added.

"Okay," she said.

She sounded like she had nothing to hide.

Edwards went out and came back with a form he kept in the police car. It was attached to a clipboard. On the top was CONSENT TO SEARCH. Giles signed her name on the bottom line and then Shanlian escorted her to his car while Melki and Edwards searched the premises.

After she stepped in, Shanlian got behind the wheel, started it up, and threw the heater on.

"I'd just like to ask you some questions about Nancy Billiter."

"Sure. Mind if I smoke?"

"No."

Giles took out a pack of cigarettes, shook one out and put it to her lips. Shanlian struck a match and lit it for her.

"Thanks," she said, exhaling smoke with a sigh.

"You're welcome. What I was wondering

about was how long Nancy had been living with you."

"Oh, for several weeks," said Carol.

Shanlian looked up.

"Looks like a small house."

"She slept on a bed in the basement," Carol explained.

"Where'd you get the coke?" Shanlian asked.

"I thought you said you weren't interested in it?"

"I'm not. I was just wondering."

"I bought it from a guy name of Hoffis Thurman in Rochester for one hundred dollars. I was taking it to my boyfriend, Tim Collier, in Flint."

Flint, thought Shanlian. Where Billiter was dumped. So there is a connection.

"Where in Flint is Collier staying?"

"Don't know," said Carol, exhaling smoke.

It was beginning to feel very warm inside the car.

"I don't know the area real well. But I could take you there," she added.

"How'd you know Nancy?" the detective asked.

"I met her through my dead husband, Jessie Giles."

She looked down for a second and then looked back up.

"He was her cocaine dealer."

"Carol, why don't you tell me what happened here?" said Shanlian gently.

Carol thought for a moment and took a long puff on her cigarette.

"Okay. On Wednesday night, Nancy got home, I don't know, around eleven. Nancy and Tim went down into the basement and were smoking crack. See, Tim was upset at Nancy."

"About what?"

Shanlian thought he knew the answer.

"A burglary that happened while Tim and me were in California on vacation."

"What happened then?"

"Nancy and Tim, they weren't fighting," Carol answered defensively, "but Tim accused her of stealing a VCR. Nancy got so upset that she called someone on the phone."

"What time was that?"

"About one-thirty. It was the middle of the night."

"Who'd she call?"

"I don't know."

"Then what happened?"

"Some guy picked her up a little while after."

"Did you get a look at him?"

"No."

"What was Nancy wearing?"

"Her burgundy work shirt, black jeans and black tennis shoes. You know, what I couldn't figure out is why she didn't take her coat with her. It was a cold night."

"Who was in the house with you on Wednesday before she left?"

"The only ones here were Nancy, Tim and my two kids, Jesse and Jesseca."

"Carol, did you murder Nancy Billiter?"

"No. No, I didn't," she answered emphatically.

Even if she did do it, he didn't expect her to admit it. But he had to ask. He'd actually had one case where someone had answered yes. You just never knew what people would do.

"Did Collier murder Nancy Billiter?"

"I don't know."

Now, that was an interesting answer, he thought.

"Carol, would you pass a lie detector test if you were asked the question 'Do you have knowledge of the murder of Nancy Billiter?' "

Carol hesitated.

"No," she said finally.

"Would you come to the West Bloomfield Township Police Department to finish this interview?"

Carol hesitated.

"It's just right down the block."

That did it. Carol agreed. They stepped outside to the marked squad car.

"Officer, would you take us over to your headquarters, please?"

"Right away, Detective," said the cop behind the wheel, who started the car up and made a U-turn.

He drove down the block. There was a big illuminated sign that said WEST BLOOMFIELD AD-

MINISTRATION COMPLEX. He turned into the driveway that led up to a big official-looking building sprawl of gray buildings in the middle of what looked like an industrial park but was actually the township's administrative center.

They parked in front of a one-story building that had a sign in silver block letters on top of the front door: WEST BLOOMFIELD TOWNSHIP POLICE DEPARTMENT.

"Thank you," Giles said politely to Shanlian, who held the door open for her. Her high heels clicking against the tiled floor in the lobby, Carol Giles stepped inside.

Four

The community's affluence had given West Bloomfield's police a state-of-the-art building, which Shanlian noticed was incredibly neat. Nothing was out of place, not a file cabinet nor a paper clip. Everything was in soft shades of white and gray, blue and green, from the cubicles the detectives occupied to the neat offices of the watch commanders. Even the interrogation room he was escorted to was neat, with a gray metal desk and a few comfortable office chairs. Soft, overhead fluorescence provided the lighting.

Carol Giles took the seat closest to the door. Sometimes, cops liked to place the suspect on the far side of the table, near the wall. That was a subtle psychological ploy, intended to make the suspect feel closed in. But Shanlian, who sat opposite her, sensed that Giles would be more talkative if she felt she could leave at any time.

Someone offered to get them drinks. Carol wanted a coffee, but Shanlian never touched the stuff. He preferred the pure caffeinated, sugary jolt of Mountain Dew.

After Carol received her coffee and an ashtray—Shanlian figuring that like many smokers she would do it under stress—the detective got down to business.

"Look, Mrs. Giles, I want to remind you that you're not a suspect and you're not under arrest," Shanlian began.

"I understand," Carol replied, sipping at her coffee.

The point of the warning was to make it clear that she could walk away anytime she wanted, that she was not under duress. The reason Shanlian didn't read her her rights, even though she was already a suspect in his mind, was that had he done so, she probably would have clammed up. He was trying to engender her trust. If he could get that, she'd open up and tell him what happened. Then he'd read her her rights; she'd write down her statement; he'd clear the case quickly; and everybody would go home happy. But he had a long way to go.

From previous interviews—cop speak for interrogations—Shanlian knew that 90 percent of what he and the suspect said in the interrogation room wouldn't even go into his report. It wasn't that he was hiding anything, far from it. Contrary to TV stereotypes, cops gain statements and confessions from suspects not by violence but by trust. So Shanlian let Carol talk.

She kept going back to her kids and how much she loved them. He lent a sympathetic ear. She relaxed. When Shanlian sensed that she was getting comfortable with him, he asked her a straight question.

"How can I find Tim Collier?"

"You take I-75 [north] to I-475, get off on the Carpenter Road exit. Then you cross the railroad tracks and drive on some side streets across from a church. He's staying someplace over there."

Right, "over there," very specific, he thought.

"Okay, what kind of car was he driving?"

"My car. A rose colored '88 Caddy DeVille."

"Plate number?"

"BPE, or maybe FMW-10."

She wasn't sure, but that was okay. He'd tap into the state's motor vehicle database and get that information. Once he had it, he could put out a bulletin to law enforcement agencies requesting Collier's apprehension.

"Mrs. Giles, you mentioned before that your husband had died. I'm sorry for your loss."

"Thank you."

"Could you tell me what he died from?"

"He had had a stroke about a year ago and he'd been in ill health ever since."

"Ill health or bad health?"

Both, it seemed. The guy was a diabetic with a heart condition. He weighed almost 500 pounds.

"I think my husband knew he was dying, because he asked me to go shopping. When I returned, he was dead."

He didn't want her to be there when death took his body.

"How long were you married?" Shanlian asked solicitously.

"Eleven years. We were together since I was fifteen."

As the conversation wore on, she got friendlier. From the way she answered questions, she sounded like a people pleaser. Shanlian sensed that someplace down the line, back in her past, Giles had been abused. Psychologically, physically, it did not matter. It made you anxious to please another human being so you wouldn't be abused further.

"Jessie, that's my husband, he treated me badly," she volunteered.

"Really?" said the cop sympathetically.

"Yeah. If one of his customers needed, you know, a favor, I was there for them."

"You mean a sexual favor?" asked Shanlian with quiet, seemingly naive interest.

"Yes."

She wasn't a prostitute, but her husband had prostituted her.

"And what business was he in?" the detective asked, knowing the answer.

"Drugs," she replied.

It was quite common for drug dealers to offer their girlfriends to regular buyers. The girlfriends agreed. It was a business arrangement.

Sex occasionally with clients, in return for being taken care of—cars, money, whatever they wanted.

Carol Giles, Shanlian felt, was the kind of woman who would tell a man what he wanted to hear. She may not have been a prostitute but in that sense, she acted like one.

"How long were you dating Tim Collier?" the detective wondered.

"Several months," she replied.

"Carol, would you pass a lie detector test if you were asked if Tim Collier had murdered Nancy Billiter?"

"I don't know."

"Are you scared of Collier?"

"Yes, yes," Carol said, practically jumping to answer that question.

"Why?"

"Timmy told me that he had done seven people, seven murders, while he was involved with a gang in Sacramento, California."

"What can you tell me about those homicides?"

"I can't remember. When me and Timmy were in Port Huron recently, he wanted to get a seven-man tattoo to represent the killings."

"What about sex? Between Nancy and Collier?"

"Nah, I don't think they were involved together."

Shanlian remembered the burn marks on Bil-

liter's body and the bong on the coffee table
in Giles's house.

"Has Tim Collier ever burned you with a
bong?"

Carol had been looking down at the table.
After the question was asked, she looked up
and began to cry.

"Tim used to use acid to do that," she
blurted out. "It's still in my car at my house.
The acid is. And," she sobbed, "Nancy and
Tim, they had been smoking crack in the basement on Wednesday night."

She looked over at Shanlian.

"Yes?"

"And they were talking about the burglary.
See, I didn't believe Nancy that a burglary had
occurred, because I found my daughter's coin
bank in the car I'd loaned to Nancy."

In Carol's mind, that meant that it was Nancy
who had stolen the VCR and other stuff and
she had made up some cock-and-bull story
about a burglar.

"What happened after Tim and Nancy smoked
crack? What time was that?"

"About eleven-thirty. Then about one-thirty,
I went upstairs to check on my children, who
were sleeping. When I got back to the basement, Nancy was on the bed, tied up with nylons, and she was screaming."

Shanlian knew that would explain the ligature marks he'd noticed on her wrists. *Now we're
getting down to it,* Shanlian thought.

"What happened then?"

"Nancy's pants leg was off."

Shanlian remembered that from the scene.

"And Tim was beating her with a .45," Carol continued.

That explained the beating and bruise marks.

"I was scared because Tim pointed the gun at me, so I went upstairs."

Now that was strange. If a guy pointed a gun at Shanlian, he'd freeze. Guy points a gun at Carol Giles and she responds by saying, "Excuse me, gotta go," and leaving the room. That just didn't make sense, unless she had more guts than any man or woman alive.

"I smoked two cigarettes upstairs and then Tim came up, and after that, I didn't hear Nancy screaming anymore. Could I use the bathroom?"

"Sure."

Shanlian got up and opened the door. He asked one of the detectives to show her to the ladies' room.

"Stand outside while she does her business," Shanlian advised.

With Carol gone, and his concentration momentarily broken, Shanlian was able to note how hot the interview room had gotten. Two bodies were in the overheated air and both reeked of sweat, one of fear. Shanlian stepped out into the corridor and ran into one of the local detectives. "I got her to open up," he said.

"We know," replied the cop.

"What?"

Shanlian was more than surprised; he was shocked. How the hell did they know what was happening inside the room? There wasn't even a two-way mirror.

Turned out there was a microphone hidden in the room. The local cops had been listening all along. They heard every single word.

For a minute, Shanlian felt violated. How dare they listen in without him knowing? Then he calmed down and realized it didn't make any difference. After all, he had gotten her to open up.

Shanlian was convinced Carol Giles knew more than she was willing to tell. She had too many details of the crime down pat for someone who was just on the scene. If she wasn't a participant, then she definitely helped dump the body.

But what to do with her now? They didn't have enough to charge her, and if they released her, they knew they would be SOL—shit out of luck. Giles could easily take a powder.

Ever since Officer Tom Helton had been promoted out of uniformed patrol and into the detective bureau a few months before, his life had gotten a lot more interesting.

Fender benders and domestic disturbances were now a thing of the past. He'd done that and the usual patrol stuff for eighteen years in uniform. Then when a position in the detective bureau opened up, he applied for it and was accepted.

Helton looked like the actor Ned Beatty had in his youth, but even more affable. He was intelligent and dedicated, and he loved his new job. It gave him a chance to investigate crimes in depth, crimes like robbery, credit card fraud and burglaries, which were common in the township.

As for murder, this wasn't a big-city police department. Sure, the chief was a retired bigwig from Detroit, but that's about as close as they got to a connection with big-city homicide.

In the eighteen years Helton had been on the force, Bloomfield averaged maybe one murder a year, and there were years when no one was murdered in the confines of the township. It was a nice, safe, secure place to live.

Like most of his friends at work, Helton couldn't afford to live in the township. He lived in the next township over, in a plain A-frame house with his wife, Doris, and their two kids, eight-year-old Al and twelve-year-old Marie.

That Friday night, he was the on-call detective. That meant that if a crime occurred after 5:00 P.M. and before 8:00 A.M., he would be called in to investigate. More often than not, things were quiet and the on-call got a good night's sleep.

Tom and his family had had dinner together.

Afterward, he puttered around the house, reading a magazine, playing with the kids; then at ten o'clock, he turned on his favorite Friday night TV show, *Homicide*. After watching the local news and a little bit of *Nightline*, he turned in around 11:45 P.M. Five minutes later, the phone rang. He sighed, the way someone sighs when they know they're about to get bad news.

"Hello?"

"Hi, this is Dispatcher Johnson at the station," said a female voice. "This Officer Helton?"

"Yup."

"Would you come in? We have a homicide. It looks like two women and a guy were partying and doing crack, some type of argument broke out and one of the women was killed."

"I'll be right there."

As he got out of bed, Doris said, "You ought to get a regular job like I have." Helton laughed, because his wife was more used to the crazy hours than he was—she ran the state's crime lab and was frequently called out to crime scenes at all hours.

Still safely ensconced under the covers, Doris asked what was up. Helton quickly explained while changing into jeans and a T-shirt. He kissed Doris good-bye. He padded quietly out and down the darkened stairs to the garage, where he started up his 1996 Ford Taurus. He pressed the gray button on the plastic case attached to the visor.

With a grinding of gears and pulleys, the garage door slowly opened and Helton pulled out into the night to help work a case that, at least according to the dispatcher, sounded like a pretty simple murder. Ten minutes later, he got to headquarters and pulled around back to the parking lot reserved for uniformed and plainclothes officers. The one out front was primarily for visitors.

"Carol Giles basically claims she was a witness to the murder of Nancy Billiter," Lieutenant Sheridan explained when Helton arrived at headquarters.

"Who'd she say did it?" asked Helton.

"Her boyfriend, Tim Collier," said Shanlian, who introduced himself and quickly sketched in the case's Genesee County background.

"She told us of some places Collier stays in when he's in Flint," Shanlian continued.

Helton knew Flint to be a real low-life city. He knew about the GM pullout and how the locals had suffered. Not surprisingly, especially to sociologists and cops, crime skyrocketed as the employment rate plummeted.

"We think he might be in Flint, and we've got my police department staking out his haunts.

"I've requested a search warrant for the Giles house and the crime lab to get down here to process it," added Sheridan.

That all made sense. The Giles house was now considered to be a crime scene.

"Here." Shanlian handed over five documents. Helton looked through the pile.

There was a consent to search form signed by Giles for the home at Walnut Lake Road; a copy of the Genesee County Medical Control Authority ambulance run #199493 (the cargo was Nancy Billiter's body); a time card and employee fact sheet for Nancy Billiter from her employer, South Boulevard Station in Auburn Hills; and two pages from a phone bill in the name of "Phyllis Burke," mother of the victim, showing eighteen phone calls to the West Bloomfield residence of Carol Giles.

Helton tagged them and placed them into evidence. While the material could not be contaminated, like forensics, it was possible for a defense lawyer to contend later that the chain of custody was somehow broken. It was therefore best to log evidence ASAP.

"Also Kate McNamara is coming down," said Sheridan.

McNamara was the on-call prosecutor for the Oakland County Prosecutor's Office. The on-call's job was to make sure the cops did everything by the book so nothing would get thrown out in court and to offer whatever assistance was necessary and appropriate. Helton knew McNamara to be a real nice lady.

Sheridan explained that they had already put out an APB on Collier, who was driving a gold-colored Caddy. Two cars, one marked, the other plain, had been sent to stake out the

Giles house in case Collier came back. The department's unmarked car was a Ford Expedition without top lights, but there were strobes inside that could be employed in an emergency.

"Sounds like we got it pretty well covered," said Helton. "Maybe I should look in on her."

"She's writing out her statement now," said Shanlian.

Helton stuck his head in the interview room and saw Carol laboring fiercely over a yellow foolscap pad.

"Want a Coke?" he asked her with a smile.

"No thanks," she answered, head up for a second, then back down to her writing.

Helton quickly closed the door.

"So what do we do with her now?" Shanlian asked.

The three men quickly reviewed what they had so far and agreed they didn't have enough to charge her. But like Shanlian said, they'd be SOL if they let her go.

"She says she was abused, right?" Helton asked.

Shanlian nodded.

"There's a battered woman's shelter nearby. It's called Haven. We can put her there overnight for safekeeping."

It was agreed to do just that. Back in the interview room, Kevin Shanlian told Carol Giles what her accommodations would be for the night, emphasizing how she would be safe there, away from Timmy and anyone else who would want to do her harm.

"Oh, thanks," said Carol, sounding relieved. She handed over her written statement. Outside, Shanlian examined it.

"Nancy was moaning and Tim hit her in the head with the gun," Carol had written. "It looked like Tim had killed her. I was scared. I didn't know what to do. I looked away from Nancy. Tim had the gun. I didn't want him to shoot me. Who would take care of Jesseca and L'il Man?"

Throughout it all, the basement TV had been on. Carol sat down on the floor next to it. She looked at the moving images on the screen and realized she hadn't been paying any attention to it, but there was something about its comforting presence, so she kept it on. She smoked two cigarettes, one after the other, trying to think about what she should do.

"If I call the police, he'll know I was on the phone and kill me before they got here. If I just made sure the kids didn't wake up and get out of bed, they'll be all right," she wrote.

As these thoughts were flooding through her mind, Tim came downstairs and turned off the TV and all the lights, except the light in the backyard and out at the garage.

"I know she did it. I know she did it,"

he kept saying. 'Bitch can't lie good. Everything's going to be all right. I'll take care of you and the kids. Everything's going to be fine.'

"I just looked at him. I didn't know what to say. He still had the gun in his hand."

Tim got up and looked out the windows.

" 'They could be out there,' Tim said. 'They know what we did. They won't come in but they know.'

" 'We didn't do anything, you did,' I answered. He turned real fast, looked at me strange, like someone had taken over his body. His eyes didn't look the same. I felt like he was looking thru [sic] me. He came over to me.

" 'We're in this together. The police won't believe I did it. I was never here. We'll take Nancy somewhere.' I was sitting on the couch, watching him pace the floor back and forth, back and forth. Before I know it, I had to get the kids up for school. It was 7:05."

She got the kids up and out for school. Carol went back to her bedroom, where Tim was smoking crack.

" 'Sit down,' he said.

"I sat next to him on the bed.

" 'I'll take Nancy for a ride. Everything will be all right,' he said.

" 'Timmy, I'm scared,' I said.

" 'Just remember, look them in the eye

and say you don't know anything. If you look them in the eye, they'll never know.'

"I just sat on the bed while he smoked. Time just went . . . on by.

" 'Come on,' he said finally.

"We went downstairs. He untied Nancy and wraped [*sic*] the blanket around her. I just stood there.

" 'Come and help me,' he said.

"I couldn't. I just stared at him. He pulled her by the legs and started towards the stairs. Her head hit the floor and she didn't scream. I almost cried out. He pulled her up the stairs. He pulled her to the garage. He put her in the trunk of my Sable. Tim acted real nervous. Fidgety. He kept smokin' crack.

" 'I'll get rid of all the evidence and the body. They'll never know.' "

They wound up going north and dumping the body in a park in Flint that he knew.

And that was Carol's statement.

After he finished reading it, Shanlian knew Carol was full of shit. It was his gut telling him that. He just knew it. But he couldn't prove it, at least not yet. One essential element had been established, though.

The murder had been committed in West Bloomfield Township, part of Oakland County and not in Flint, part of Genesee County. The county where the murder took place had venue in the investigation and prosecution. That meant the ball was now in West Bloomfield's and Oakland County's court, literally and figuratively.

Flint had more than its fair share of homicides; the force was already overworked. In just the brief time he'd been in West Bloomfield, Shanlian had discovered that homicides were rare. The locals were really looking forward to working the case.

At 2:00 A.M., Kevin Shanlian officially turned the case over to Helton and the West Bloomfield Police Department.

"Whatever you need on my end, just let me know," Shanlian told Helton.

"Will do."

Driving north on the interstate, Shanlian was weary. He needed sleep. But he was a good detective; his mind kept working. He needed to know who had actually killed Nancy Billiter.

And why. He was convinced it wasn't because Tim suspected Nancy of faking a burglary. There had to be another reason. There had to be.

Otherwise, human life was just too damn cheap.

Back in West Bloomfield, Carol Giles was thinking nothing of the sort. Actually, she wasn't thinking at all, at least consciously.

Police officers had checked her into Haven. She found the place to be exactly that. Once she put her head down on the pillow in her rather large room, she slept and slept and slept.

Five

A search warrant was quickly obtained for Carol Giles's car. At the Giles house, Helton entered the garage area. There was a Caddy there; he found nothing of value inside. Outside, Carol's Sable was still in the driveway. Helton searched it and made a list of what he found:

1. From the center area between the two front seats, I found a white plastic container that contained battery acid. It was about 1/6th full.

2. Just in front of the container of acid, under some napkins, I found a loaded .32 Caliber Titan. It was unloaded by removing the loaded magazine and also taking a round from the chamber.

3. In the drivers side vassar I found written directions to a road near Flint.

4. Under the drivers seat I found the victims drivers license.

5. In the trunk, I found an empty red gas can.

6. In the trunk I found suspected blood on the floor carpet. The whole floor carpet was removed.

After removing the items from the vehicle, Helton carefully bagged, tagged and secured them. A copy of the search warrant tabulation was made out and left in the vehicle.

Officers Duncan and Renaldo were lounging in their patrol car on Main Street in Flint when they saw the gold-colored Cadillac go by. There was a young black man behind the wheel. Something about him and the car looked familiar to Renaldo, but he couldn't figure out what it was.

About an hour later, the car went by again. This time it was Duncan who noticed it, because his partner was catching a few winks. It looked familiar to him, too.

The guy hadn't broken any laws. There wasn't any need, let alone reason, to stop him. Of course, had the two officers remembered the APB they had received earlier in the evening on a gold-colored Cadillac being driven by a young black man named Tim Collier, who was wanted in connection with a murder down in West Bloomfield Township—well, they certainly would have stopped him.

* * *

Parked in the driveway of the Giles house, Officer Ralph Sampson felt lonely. Usually he had Rollo, the department's German shepherd, to keep him company.

Sampson was the department's canine officer. Usually it was just he and Rollo on a case. But he'd been drafted into service because he happened to be in the office at the time the call came in. Rollo, meanwhile, was back at the kennel, happily sleeping through the night. That sounded good, being in bed at home, instead of staking out a house, waiting for a suspect to come back, who probably . . .

He saw the headlights in his rearview mirror. They approached slowly, down the east side of the street, then turned in. The car parked right behind him. Car doors slammed. Two guys came out of the gold-colored Caddy.

"Hey, what the hell you doing—"

"Police," said Sampson.

The short, handsome man looked behind him and saw a marked police car pull in behind his Caddy.

"Are you Tim Collier?" Sampson asked.

"Yeah, what's this—"

"Put your hands on the car and spread your legs."

"Hey!" said the guy Collier was with.

"Hey, *sir,*" said Sampson, who kicked Collier's feet apart, frisked him quickly, and then snapped on the cuffs.

"Hey, sir, what's—"

"Check this guy out and if he's clean, let him go," said Sampson to the two uniforms. Collier was hustled over to the unmarked car, while the uniforms checked on Tim's companion.

Over at the unmarked vehicle, Sampson pushed Tim's head down, ensuring it didn't hit the top of the car, into the backseat behind the chicken wire.

"There's some people who'd like to talk to you, Tim."

"Really?" said Collier.

"Yeah," said Sampson, smiling down at him from outside the car, "and they've been waiting all night."

Sampson pulled out, but the marked car stayed at the scene. Inside it, the central processing unit (CPU) in a portable computer hummed. It was tied into a mainframe at headquarters a few blocks away.

The name of Tim's companion was John Ellis. The uniforms had punched Ellis's name in. They were waiting for the readout. The CPU hummed and clicked and onto the screen came John Ellis's record:

- Failure to Appear—$100 Bond
- Non-Moving Traffic Violation—$100 Bond
- Non-Moving Traffic Violation—$100 Bond
- Failure to Appear—$150 Bond
- Non-Moving Traffic Violation—$100 Bond
- Non-Moving Traffic Violation—$100 Bond
- Non-Moving Traffic Violation—$500 Bond

"Looks like you were hanging out with the wrong guy at the wrong time," said one of the uniforms. He put Ellis in the car for transport to police headquarters.

"Why am I being arrested?" Ellis asked as the car took off.

One of the uniforms looked at the screen.

"How about five unpaid tickets and two failures to appear?"

"You're taking me in for that?"

Then Ellis thought a minute.

"Was there a murder, killing, beating or what?"

The two uniforms in the front seat looked at each other.

"Man, whatever he did, it must have been bad," Ellis said ruefully.

Helton had walked into the outer vestibule. Bulletproof glass covered the processing station at the front. Behind it sat two cops at desks who acted as receptionists. They answered calls and began prisoner processing.

As Helton watched, the large double doors to the parking lot opened. Sampson walked in with a handcuffed Tim Collier and escorted him into the detective area on the left for fingerprinting and mug shots.

In his many years as a street cop, Helton had seen all kinds of people—druggies, prostitutes, killers. There were also all kinds in each category, and sometimes, there was something about a suspect, something indefinable, that you couldn't put your finger on.

Despite Collier's muscular build and handsome, chiseled features, his stature—five feet six inches—did not make him look particularly dangerous. No, it was the air about him, the vibe he gave off.

Helton had seen some guys who cultivated it, bad guy wanna-bes who were better off going to Hollywood than trying to make it on the street. Collier, though, was different. He was the genuine article; he felt mean.

They took Collier to the same interview room previously occupied by his lover and read him Carol's written statement. He showed little outward reaction. Inside, he must have been boiling.

"Did you kill Nancy Billiter?" Helton asked.

"Why would I kill her?" he countered.

"Do you know of any reason why Carol Giles would accuse you of murdering Nancy Billiter?"

"No. But I want to hear Carol say that at trial."

"Did Giles participate in this murder and should she be held?"

"That's for you to find out."

Tim said that he didn't want to answer any more questions about the murder until he talked to an attorney. Eventually, though, he relented and gave police this written statement:

"Carol, Nancy and I were sitting in her basement. Me and Nancy were getting high, we were loading our stems (get high equipment) when Carol told Nancy that she thought she was the one who ripped her off, reason being that we found the piggy bank in the trunk of Carol's car and also knowing that the person Nancy suspected of breaking in was too fat to go or reach through that doors amongst all that glass. Nancy kept saying she loved Carol; and she thought they were closer than that and she wouldn't do anything like that. Carol hit her with the piggy bank and dazed her. I continued getting high and walked towards the Ping-Pong table where the cat was at and took a couple of hits and walked back over to wear [sic] Carol was in the process of tying her off with the pantyhose and asked, what do she do next and I told her 'handle your business.' Nancy kept saying 'I love you,' he has come between us and something to that nature and me and Carol told her to shut up. Carol injected bleach and battery acid into Nan and then when she realized it was taking too long for her to die, a wet towel was placed over her face to suffocate her to death. When she was dead, we put her in the trunk of Carol's car and put the mattresses in the garage and that night, I helped her get rid of Nancy's body in Flint."

Tim Collier

Great, Helton thought after reading it. Now they had both suspects pointing the finger at each other. Which one was telling the truth?

In Tim's version, Carol wasn't some innocent, abused waif. If you believed him, Tim said it was Carol who injected Nancy with acid, which accounted for the burn marks on the victim's skin. As for Carol, she didn't mention the injections at all.

Helton liked to go to the movies and he remembered an old Japanese film called *Rashomon,* where a woman was raped and three witnesses had three different versions of the event. Who was telling the truth? Unfortunately in the Billiter murder, life appeared to be imitating art.

Was Carol telling the truth or Tim? Maybe, neither? It still didn't make sense. Damn it.

Why?

Nancy must have been killed for a reason. There had to be a reason. And why the damn acid? Tim had a gun. Why not just shoot her?

Detectives look for three things with which to obtain a conviction—motive, means and opportunity. The latter two criteria had already been taken care of. But the motive? That was unclear from both accounts.

In Tim's version, Nancy had faked a burglary and, because of that, she deserved to die. Did that make sense? Sure, people had been murdered for doing less, a lot less. Hell, people had been murdered for giving dirty looks. But was that the case here?

If the murder wasn't planned, certainly the body disposal was. Billiter didn't just happen to be dumped in a park in Flint over an hour away. And she didn't just happen to be covered with gasoline with a fuse of charred leaves meant to light her up like the Fourth of July. That was probably one thing they could be thankful for—neither suspect had any sort of pyrotechnic ability. Had they, the coroner would have been stuck with a corpse burned beyond recognition and cops know how difficult it is to get an ID out of one of those.

Did it make sense, Helton wondered, that the murder itself would be committed without some foresight? It was time to talk to Giles again and see what she was hiding. Maybe they could turn her against Collier.

Helton looked at his watch: 3:45 A.M. By now, Carol was probably asleep in Haven. They'd have to wait until morning to talk to her.

Officer Jim Fedorenko of the township forensic crew got to the Giles home at 3:27 A.M. The Michigan State Police (MSP) techies arrived soon after, straight from the crime scene in Flint.

"Here you go," said one of the MSP lab boys. He handed over Nancy's clothing and the flowered blanket she'd been found in. Nancy's clothing reeked of gasoline. Fedorenko's nose wrinkled up at the stench. He bagged the clothing as evidence and then began the grim task of gathering evidence.

Unless Fedorenko needed them, MSP could call it a night. Fedorenko thanked them, and they left. Using the search warrant that a local magistrate had given him, he and his search crew entered the house.

Fedorenko took out his camera. Using five rolls of film, he shot the entire interior of the house. Afterward, he collected two samples of blood spatter he found on the basement wall and one sample from the top of a table located near the blood-spattered wall.

Moving out to the garage, he looked up and saw a mattress in the rafters. What the hell was that doing there? He had the search crew take it down. Examining it, Fedorenko removed one side of the outer cover of the mattress. It was the side that contained blood and what looked like other types of fluids.

On a large round table in the living room, he found a plastic bag that contained an off-white hard substance that he suspected was the crack Tim had been smoking at the time of the murder. Crack, of course, is a deadly drug, but it doesn't produce immediate physical devastation, not like the weapon he found in the master bedroom closet.

It was a shiny 12-gauge shotgun. Ever since it had become the weapon of choice for bad guys on TV, ordinary citizens had been buying them in droves. It was the sound that attracted the buyers. It was a hard, cold snap, the sound of a shell being loaded into the chamber that sent chills up any burglar's spine.

Fedorenko broke it open and sniffed. It wasn't loaded and it had not been fired recently.

Nothing in either suspect's statement led anyone to believe it was involved in the crime. Still, considering that the residents of the house might not be back for a long time—at least he hoped so—Fedorenko thought it prudent to collect the weapon for safekeeping.

He carefully tabulated what had been taken and left that, plus a copy of the search warrant, on the dining room table. He had tow trucks come by to pick up the cars. By the time he got back to headquarters, it was 8:29 A.M.

Fedorenko secured the evidence in evidence lockers designed for that specific purpose, and the vehicles involved—Carol's Sable and Jessie's Caddy—were secured in the garage by locking them and placing yellow police tape around them.

The gas-soaked clothing, a shirt, a pair of jeans, two socks, women's panties and a black shoe, as well as the blanket, were hung up to dry. From the blanket, Fedorenko cut out a sample, which was put into a can for further testing.

***

November 15, 1977

He had arrived home too late the night before to do anything about it, but he knew the office would be open early, even on Saturday mornings.

At 7:00 A.M., Shanlian called the admitting office at Hurley Hospital, where Nancy's body had been taken. He told them the victim's name and that the body was located in the hospital morgue.

At 8:00 A.M., Shanlian got Grant Williams, the county medical examiner, on the phone. He told him that Oakland County had venue in the case and that the body would be released to Dr. Dragovic, the Oakland County medical examiner.

Late that morning, the body was transferred to the ME's headquarters in Pontiac for autopsy.

Carol awoke late morning on Saturday. About noon, a staff member knocked and then popped her head through the door of her room.

"You okay? Like to talk?" the staffer asked brightly.

Carol declined the offer and said nothing else.

"I'll be around if you need to talk," she said, and closed the door behind her.

Carol only left her room to get something to

eat and smoke a few cigarettes. She interacted with no one, appearing to many of the residents to be withdrawn. One resident, curious at this new arrival, did happen to approach her and ask, "Hey, how come you have such a large room?"

"Because I might pick up my two children to come here also," Carol explained.

She never mentioned why she was really there, or that it might be a very long time before she saw her kids again. While Carol engaged in whatever rationalizations were necessary for her to get through the day, Tom Helton was busy.

Helton went to the prosecutor's office and presented all of the information they had to that point. Kate McNamara, the on-call prosecutor, wanted Carol to take a polygraph. While not admissible in court, police look at it as an accurate method of assessing the veracity of a suspect's story. But with its low crime rate, West Bloomfield Township really had no reason to maintain such a sophisticated polygraph setup. The Oakland County Sheriff's Department, which covered the entire county, did. Helton contacted them to set up a polygraph for Carol Giles.

During a polygraph, systems of measurements are taken that measure the body's response to a series of questions. The questions that make the subject want to lie create a psychological emergency. In turn, that results in changes to the autonomic nervous system: respiration, galvanic skin response, relative blood pressure and pulse. Those changes are noted and evaluated by the polygraph examiner, who then tells the detective where the suspect has been truthful and where the suspect has lied.

Unfortunately, it was Saturday. The Sheriff's Office didn't have a polygraph examiner on duty. Helton had never been in this situation before and didn't know where to get one. He'd have to figure that out later. He needed to get Carol. Helton drove over to Haven to pick her up and soon ran into trouble.

The women who availed themselves of the shelter's services did so because they had been battered and had a problem with trust. Haven, in turn, felt a responsibility to keep their clients' names confidential. They wouldn't confirm or deny that any one person was there, even to the police.

"But this is a murder case," Helton explained to an administrator, "and I brought this woman, Carol Giles, here myself last night."

The administrator explained that that didn't make any difference. "But we brought her here last night," Helton complained to one of Haven's officials. "She's a suspect in a homicide investigation!"

"Sorry," said the official. "We can't let you in. It's against the rules."

"How about just calling her and telling her to come out here and meet us? We're the police. We're not the batterers. We brought her here for safety."

The official shook his head. He wouldn't even confirm for Helton that Carol Giles was there. Helton squared his shoulders. Striding deliberately out into the corridor, he pulled out his cell phone and dialed.

"You've reached Haven," said the operator who answered his call. "May I help you?"

"Yes, this is Officer Tom Helton of the West Bloomfield Township Police Department. I'd like to talk to Carol Giles. She's one of your residents."

"We don't take messages here for residents."

"Well, can you give her a message to call me? I'm out front and—"

"Look, Officer Helton, I can't even acknowledge she's here."

"Well, I need to contact her. What will you do?"

"We'll post a message on the bulletin board," the receptionist explained. "If she gets it, she gets it, if she doesn't, she doesn't."

"That's not gonna work! That's not good enough."

Damn.

Helton called Kate McNamara, the prosecutor, who, in turn, called the director of Haven. After haggling and negotiating, eventually they got Carol to call Helton on his cell phone. Helton identified himself and told her he was out front on his cell phone.

"Carol, please come out. We need to talk to you."

If she didn't come out, Helton probably would have had to get a warrant for her arrest. They still wanted to go soft on her until they knew exactly what happened, but if it became necessary, hard would have to do just as well.

Luck, though, was with them.

Finally, Carol came out front. Helton met her and introduced her to a uniformed deputy who, he said, would escort her to police headquarters. After she left, Helton went home.

Helton had been on duty for twenty-four hours. He was no good to anyone if he couldn't think because of exhaustion. While he settled into his bed for some much-needed rest, his supervisor, Sergeant Mike Messina, would be taking over.

Six

Because of various regulations requiring detectives to rotate back to uniformed duty, plus retirements, there was no man or woman in the West Bloomfield Township detective division with more than two years of experience in investigations. Most, actually, had less.

Mike Messina was the exception.

Messina was a veteran, or a dinosaur, depending on your point of view. What was undeniable was the man's experience.

By the time Jessie Giles had blown into town, Mike Messina had been a police officer for twenty-five of his forty-seven years. Since 1982 he'd been a detective. He was the go-to guy when a problem came up and experience was needed.

Relaxing at home with a cup of coffee on that Saturday, Messina was sitting at his kitchen table, reading the paper, when the phone rang. Still studying the Pistons stats from the game the night before, Messina picked up the phone.

"Hello?"

It was the chief. After briefing Messina on

the case, he told him that the next step was getting Carol Giles hooked up to a polygraph. Messina hung up the phone and began to think.

West Bloomfield wasn't Detroit, where they had murders all the time and polygraph examiners available twenty-four hours. Where was Messina supposed to get a polygraph examiner in an affluent, safe Detroit suburb on a Saturday? Messina realized he needed a favor, but from whom?

The answer was Chester Romatowski.

Chet was an old acquaintance of Messina's. He was a polygraph examiner affiliated with the Oakland County Sheriff's Department (OCSD). He called Chet at home and explained the situation. Immediately, Chet volunteered to help.

Messina briefed Romatowski on the case so he could tailor his questions accordingly. They were interested principally in the extent of Carol's involvement with the killing and the disposal of the body. Messina arranged to meet him at the OCSD polygraph office in Pontiac. He then had a deputy transport Carol to Pontiac for the test.

L. J. Dragovic looked down at the naked body on the cold metal of the autopsy table. His skilled hands moved over it, examining, probing.

As the chief medical examiner for Oakland

County, he had most recently tried to nail Dr. Jack Kevorkian for helping to administer lethal doses of carbon monoxide to Merian Frederick and Dr. Ali Khalili. And failed. Or at least the system had; Kevorkian had been found not guilty at trial in March 1996.

Now, Dragovic put all that out of his mind and noted that Billiter's nostrils contained a large amount of dried blood, and the nose itself looked like it had been hit by something. Her lips were split from injury; her mouth contained dried blood. Neck, chest and abdomen also had been injured.

When he turned her over, he saw that her anus and lower extremities had been traumatized. Her body had been doused with some gasolinelike chemical.

Both of Nancy's hands had been covered with plastic bags at the scene, which Dragovic now removed. He noted that her hands had a moderate "washerwoman's hands" appearance.

Samples of combed and pulled scalp and pubic hair were taken, along with fingernail clippings. Oral, vaginal and rectal smears were also taken. If Billiter had been sodomized, and the perpetrator ejaculated, it should show up on a DNA analysis.

Going back for a more careful examination, Dragovic noted "blunt force trauma" on the right side of the forehead, right temple, right ear and back of the head with bleeding into the subcutaneous tissue of the scalp. The right eye socket was bruised, with swelling and bruising of the right cheekbone.

There was extensive bruising of the left eye socket, too, extending into the left cheekbone with marked swelling of the face in the area. There was a three-quarter-inch-long patterned tear of the skin on the left side of the lower part of the forehead. Another one-half-inch-long tear of the scalp was observed in the upper part of the left side of the forehead.

Farther down on the face, Billiter's nose had been fractured and the skin scraped at various points. There were also extensive scrapes on the left side of the lower face extending into the left side of the chin. Both upper and lower lips were torn extensively, with bruising of the front parts of the upper and lower gums. As for her mouth, there was a large amount of aspirated (thrown up) blood in the upper and lower airways.

Along the extremities, hands, arms and wrists had been bruised extensively and in some places, the skin torn. Her belly had a bruise and the right lower chest area, too. There was dried blood within and around the anus with superficial tearing, indicative of sodomy. That is, sodomy while the victim was alive.

Dead bodies do not bleed. If she had been sodomized after death, there would have been no bleeding. But there was and that's how Dragovic knew it had happened while she was alive. That didn't mean, however, that the sodomy did not extend *into* death. The perpetrator could have penetrated her prior to death and then continued after she died. They wouldn't know that until, at least, someone was held responsible for the crime.

Moving back across the body, Dragovic discovered fractures of the right seventh through eleventh ribs. Then he noted "sharp force injury." There was an almost one-inch-deep cut in the "inner aspect of the left thumb." As for the strange discoloring on her arms that the cops had noted at the scene, Dragovic solved that mystery quickly.

"There are multiple areas of injection sites," he wrote in his autopsy report, "featuring superficial and deep chemical burns situated in the right and left sides of the neck, upper mid belly area, and mid lower and left belly areas, inner aspect of the right thigh, right lower groin and outside aspect of the right thigh as well as inner aspect of the right lower leg."

He felt the neck and examined it closely. There was a hemorrhage into the soft tissue on both sides in relation to the puncture wounds. The larynx and trachea contained a large amount of blood.

Using a drill and saw, Dragovic cut through Billiter's scalp and skull, eventually lifting off the skullcap. He noted "mild cortical swelling" but no fractures.

Cutting into her trunk, Dragovic probed the body cavity. He found blood in the bronchial tubes, caused by the blunt trauma to the face and the resultant bleeding. The liver, biliary tract, spleen, lymph nodes, pancreas, enitourinary system and gastrointestinal tract were all normal. The stomach contained about 200 milliliters of fluid with identifiable pieces of rice and brown beans.

Rice and beans. That had been Nancy Billiter's last meal before she was murdered.

Back at the scene, Detective Shanlian had not been qualified to comment on "cause of death," but Dragovic certainly was. Under DIAGNOSIS in his report, he wrote:

1. Asphyxia due to oxygen deprivation
2. Multiple blunt force injuries
3. Multiple acid injection burns

Under OPINION, Dragovic stated:

"This 45-year-old white female, Nancy Billiter, died of asphyxia due to oxygen deprivation brought about by aspiration of blood into the upper and lower airways resulting from blunt force trauma of the face/nose and blockage of the upper airways by gagging.

"The decedent was beaten, bound, gagged and tortured by multiple injections of caustic chemical (acid) into the soft tissues. There was no evidence of pre-existing disease. The decedent was under the influence of cocaine at the time of sustaining the above-described injuries. In consideration of the circumstances surrounding this death, the results of this postmortem examination and the toxicological analysis, the manner of death is homicide."

Put another way, Nancy Billiter had been smothered to death but not before someone coldly beat and carefully tortured her. Beatings in homicide cases are common, but torture is unusual. That left police with questions: Who tortured her and why? Was it a sadistic killer or someone trying to elicit information, or maybe some combination of the two? Maybe it was a serial killer that didn't feel anything but exacted pleasure by hurting women?

A quick check of law enforcement databases showed no similar modus operandi among active unsolved homicides believed to have been committed by serial killers. Then why was Nancy Billiter tortured before she died? It was up to the primary detective on the case to answer those questions.

Dragovic picked up the phone and called the detective bureau in West Bloomfield Township. He got on the line with Mike Messina. The cop and the coroner had a fruitful conversation.

An hour later, Chester Romatowski walked in the doors of the OCSD. Carol Giles was already waiting for him. He took her into the polygraph examining room. He explained how the polygraph worked. He read her the Miranda warning. Carol agreed to waive her rights and signed a statement to that effect. The waiver, though, could be superseded if the suspect verbally asked for an attorney. If that happened, the interview had to cease immediately. If it didn't, anything she said after that could not be used in court against her.

Romatowski interviewed her and obtained the same version of the story she had told Shanlian the night before. Finally he hooked her up to the machine. With wires attached to her body, the other ends to the machine, Romatowski explained, "Not telling the whole truth will result in your not passing the polygraph."

Suddenly, Carol looked worried. She hadn't looked good when they started, but now she looked positively sick.

"Is there something wrong?" Romatowski asked.

Carol said nothing. It must have felt like the world was closing in on her.

"Are you withholding any information?"

Nothing.

"Do you want to speak to an attorney?"

"I want to speak to an attorney!" Carol blurted out.

It was as close to a constitutional crisis as the average cop ever gets. What do you do when the suspect says she wants a lawyer and you know if the lawyer comes in the suspect will clam up? You cannot deny the suspect that privilege. However, there's nothing in the statute that says you cannot offer the suspect a choice.

Thinking fast, Romatowski answered, "You may speak to an attorney if you wish or you can speak to a detective."

Carol paused to think. Romatowski seemed like a nice guy. So did the cops the night before. They were easy to talk to and she had some things she needed to get off her chest.

"I want to talk to the detective," she said finally.

Messina had arrived and was outside the polygraph room. He was surprised when Chet came out with Carol so quickly. Romatowski introduced them.

"Mrs. Giles. Hi, I'm Sergeant Messina," he said with a smile and an extended hand.

They shook hands awkwardly.

"Sergeant," Romatowski explained, "we didn't do the test."

Uh-oh. Messina had learned long ago when you didn't know what to say, say nothing.

"Carol didn't think she'd pass it," Romatowski continued. "She would like to talk to you."

Messina felt relieved. He smiled easily.

"Why don't we talk down here?" he offered, leading the way with an outstretched arm to the interview room in the investigators' bureau down the hall. While Carol seated herself, Messina spoke with Romatowski briefly.

"Thanks, Chet," he said and closed the door.

He sat down across from Carol and reviewed the case file that he had brought with him. He saw that Timmy Collier had been arrested and charged with Nancy Billiter's murder. Carol's story was something like, "Yeah, I was there when it happened; He was riled and on coke. He held a gun on me and made me help him in some ways."

She was a witness to a murder, Messina felt, and her veracity needed to be determined before they put her on the stand. The hope was that she would testify against Tim. Unfortunately, she couldn't. At least, not yet.

By her own admission, she couldn't pass a polygraph. What was she leaving out? *Something isn't making sense here*, thought Messina.

He was convinced that the reason she wouldn't take the polygraph was that she was more involved in Nancy's murder than she was letting on. She was probably worried that the polygraph would trip her up.

"Okay, Carol, we're going to go over this one more time with you," Messina began. "What I'd like you to do is before we start—first I want to ask you, do you know you're being taped at this time?"

"Yes," Carol answered, looking down at the tape recorder that Messina had just turned on.

"Okay, and it's with your permission?"

"It's fine," she answered.

Once more, Messina went over her Miranda

rights, the speech anyone who has ever watched a police show can recite verbatim. Except that in real life, after the cop reads the suspect her rights, the suspect signs a waiver that she has been informed and is waiving those rights. That way, the suspect can never claim she didn't know what she was doing. It was actually the second waiver Carol signed that day, the first for the polygraph that never took place.

"Okay, I'm gonna witness it," said Messina, signing next to her name. Then he looked at his watch. "The time is 6:10 P.M."

Messina now adopted the posture of sympathetic listener. No matter what he thought of her personally, whether she was a scumbag or an abused woman caught in the middle, he had to treat her sympathetically. Otherwise, she'd clam up.

"Do you need a rest room, or if you'd like to get something to eat? Do you feel okay?"

"I'm fine," Carol reassured him.

"Okay, then, fine. I'd like you to tell me what happened regarding the death of Nancy. Start at the beginning and just tell it like it was. I want you to make sure that you don't leave out anything regarding what happened before or after, so make sure that you include everything in your statement. First, before we start, I want you to tell me what your full name is."

"Carol Lynn Giles."

"And, Carol, what is your date of birth?"

"November 4 of '71."

Only twenty-six and already involved in a murder.

Inside, the detective shook his head in weary acceptance. Outside, he remained emotionless. He had seen all too many women who, for one reason or another, pick the wrong people to partner with.

"Okay, how do you feel now? Physically, are you okay?"

Translation: Have we beaten you in any way? Or, are you too ill to talk?

"Physically, I'm fine."

"All right, go ahead and start, Carol."

Good cops really listen and Messina was one of the best.

Listening intently, he realized that this wasn't a simple case. Forget about how easy it was to identify the body. Figuring out who did exactly what, and why, that was going to be the real challenge.

PART TWO

PART TWO

Seven

When she was younger, Carol claimed, her dad molested her. That had been a long time ago. Yet with all those years between then and now, when her father touched her, she still didn't feel comfortable.

Carol was so scarred that even today, there was no way she'd go to her dad's house in Port Huron, north and east of Detroit, unless there was someone else accompanying her. She hated the son of a bitch. She wanted her father dead.

She'd fantasized about the details, but so far, it was still fantasy. The problem with making it into reality was that there might be other people around when it was done. What then?

Tim always said you never leave witnesses. Which brought her right back to Jessie. It was in 1986 when fifteen-year-old Carol met Jessie Giles who, at the time, was thirty-three years old.

Carol had begun to rebel during her early teenage years. She had to, to survive the horrors of home. But she took a teenager's rebellion a step further, repudiating her middle-class white father and upbringing by taking up with a black man.

At six feet tall and 468 pounds, Jessie was a big, proud black man. To Carol, he was the father she never had. To Jessie, Carol was the daughter he wanted. Their own personal neuroses fit together nicely.

Jessie managed Carol like she was his daughter. Though they didn't marry until 1993, Carol would eventually function not only as his wife but also as his business associate.

Jessie worked in maintenance at Mercy Hospital in Pontiac, but that was his day job; the vocation that netted him the easy money was dealing drugs. According to Carol, she helped out on some of his business dealings, going so far as to sleep with clients to cement deals. The latter is not an uncommon occurrence in drug-dealing circles.

If she had any sense of self, Carol would have bailed. But her sense of self had apparently been destroyed by incest. In turn, incest had left her with a strong sense of survival. Carol did what she needed to get by from day to day.

And sex was different. If Jessie got on top of her and started pumping, all that weight would crush her chest. She wouldn't be able to breathe.

So they made love . . . carefully.

Carol and Jessie had two children. Jesseca was born in 1990. Then came Jesse, nicknamed "L'il Man," born two years later in 1992. By all accounts, Carol was a good mother. The kids, of course, didn't help the marriage. They never do when a marriage is built on unfulfilled childhood desires.

As the years went by, Jessie's health deteriorated. His unchecked obesity led to diabetes, and circulation and heart problems. He suffered through a heart attack and a stroke. Eventually he was forced to leave his day job and go on disability.

Between his health and his weight, Jessie became bedridden. He looked like a beached whale under the cover of their bed. Reduced to playing nursemaid, Carol delivered Jessie's injections every day. It was her responsibility to make sure he got the proper amount of insulin to keep his disease in check. She also had to administer his other medications.

As Jessie's health failed, so did their marriage.

Jessie kept bothering her, telling her what to do, what to say, what to think. Sure, everyone that met him liked him. Jessie was charming with company. But when the door closed at midnight, he became a dictator.

Carol was an attractive twenty-six-year-old blonde, tall, slim, with a damn good body and a sweet smile. Attractive designer glasses framed her eyes. She was vibrant, alive. She wanted to be with someone who, like her, wanted to enjoy life in big gulps. Instead, she gave injections to a husband who treated her like a daughter.

She had married her father, or a man like him, who abused her, if not physically, then emotionally. Because of her childhood problems, she wasn't aware how she had set herself up for the marriage to fail. But that's exactly what was happening.

Eventually, Carol and Jessie fought all the time. Every little word they said to each other started an argument. Jessie was always telling her what to do and she hated it. Jessie just didn't understand that she wasn't his daughter.

Probably, Jessie didn't care. He had his drug business to be concerned about. And he was upwardly mobile. He wanted to move away from Pontiac, a middle-class/working-class area twenty miles northwest of Detroit, a place best known for a white elephant of an indoor football stadium, the Silverdome. The goal was to relocate south, to one of the more affluent Detroit suburbs.

Jessie Giles had an incredible amount of nerve. But not just ordinary nerve—abject nerve. The kind of nerve you need when you're a drug dealer and decide to set up shop within eyeshot of police headquarters.

That's exactly what Jessie Giles had done.

In the summer of 1997, Jessie moved his family south, into the fancy suburb of West Bloomfield. The home he chose was a quarter of a mile down Walnut Lake Road from West Bloomfield Township Police Headquarters. Who would ever think to look for him there? What could possibly be a safer place to do his business than a few blocks down from police headquarters?

Besides, he wasn't wanted for anything. Compared to the big guys in Detroit, he was small potatoes. What harm was he doing to the township? The cops had better things to do than bust him.

Only doctors, lawyers, stockbrokers or drug dealers raking it in could afford West Bloomfield. When the cops left work, they drove home to Novi or South Lyon, less affluent suburbs with more crime, smaller lawns and lower property values. Jessie, meanwhile, stayed in the township and enjoyed his new life.

Inside his new house—Jessie was actually renting because it's difficult for a drug dealer, with undeclared income, to get a mortgage—he admired his surroundings. It was much nicer than Pontiac was. As for the cops down the block, Jessie had to smile.

For Carol, the move didn't make any difference. Her discontent just rose in proportion to their affluence. She wanted out of the marriage, but she didn't know where to go.

Where could she go if she left Jessie? If she left him, what would happen to the kids? He couldn't take care of them, in the shape he was in. But Lord, she was strangling!

Carol had had enough.

What with Jessie and the responsibilities of taking care of the kids, Carol had no life. She needed to get out; she was desperate to get out. She felt like she'd murder somebody if she didn't. So Carol got a job as an office assistant at St. Joseph Mercy Hospital, Jessie's former employer. That was where she made the acquaintance of Timothy Orlando Collier, a member of the hospital maintenance staff and one of Jessie's customers who loved crack.

Tim was not exactly short, but he wasn't tall, either. What he was, at a little over five feet six inches tall, was incredibly well built and handsome, with the kind of smooth, café au lait skin that made Carol tingle all over her body.

After meeting Tim at the hospital, Carol would go over to his house to hang out all the time. For example, when she and Jessie got into it, she would go over to Tim's house to mellow out. And they would sit around and talk.

Tim talked about his troubled life growing up in Sacramento, California. He alluded to a gang background and to the violent crimes he'd committed. It was a hard life he had been born into, which had forced him into things.

Because he and his mom didn't get along, he escaped by getting high on drugs. Eventually he had come east. He had relatives in the Flint area, most notably his uncle Sammy Upchurch, whom he liked a lot.

Tim was everything Jessie wasn't—young, vital, exciting. He was a real macho guy who didn't take shit off anyone. Carol fell for him. Hard. She liked to push against his hard body.

He pushed back and soon they were lovers. The best thing was, he didn't tell her what to do all the time.

September 28, 1997

Carol had just come home from shopping when she found Jessie, unconscious, by the side of their bed. She picked up the phone and dialed. It was 2:00 P.M.

"He's so cold," Carol told the 911 operator. "I think he's, you know, I think he's already dead. He's cold."

"Well, just lay him on his back the best you can," the operator repeated for the third or fourth time.

With the help of her landlord and his son, they were finally able to get Jessie, all 468 pounds of him, on his back. The operator told her to start CPR. Carol held his nose, opened his mouth, and almost threw up.

There was something really gross in his throat. She couldn't be sure what it was, maybe some sort of puke. Ugh!

Carol heard sirens. Squealing brakes. Heavy feet pounding on pavement. The cop seemed to be by her side not more than a few seconds later. She stopped the CPR and told the operator that the police were there.

A moment later, the paramedics ran in, put their equipment down, tore Jessie's pajama top open, and attached EKG leads. While checking the digital readout, a medic asked Carol the last time she saw him conscious.

Carol told them that the last time she'd seen Jessie alive was eleven o'clock. She had gone out shopping, and when she returned, she had found him unconscious and propped up on one elbow beside the bed.

She said that Jessie seemed like he was going to have a heart attack and he wanted her to leave the house. He wanted to be alone. The implication was he knew the end was near and wanted to die alone, with dignity.

"There's no heartbeat," the medic said finally, withdrawing the leads from Jessie's bare chest. His skin was ice cold and rigor mortis had begun. The guy looked up at Carol.

"Looks like he's been dead for a while," he said sympathetically.

The medic asked Carol a few questions about Jessie's overall health. She told him about the stroke, heart attack, and diabetes. The medic called North Oakland Medical Center and relayed that information to a doctor on duty, who declared Jessie officially dead.

One of the cops gathered up all of Jessie's medications to list in his report; then he called the medical examiner, which was standard procedure in Michigan whenever a police officer arrived at the scene of a death. It didn't mean an autopsy, of course. It was, obvious to everyone present that Jessie had died of natural causes.

Carol watched as the death professionals shared the information about Jessie's health history and medications. An hour later, the man from the medical examiner's arrived. He was the ME on duty. He did a cursory examination of Jessie's body, still on the floor where he had fallen. He announced that, coupled with what they knew about his medical conditions, Jessie had died from a heart attack.

The state released the body. Carol had to call to have the body picked up. She looked through the phone book and found the name of a funeral home nearby. She called and they said they'd be right by to pick him up.

It was dark by the time the guys from the funeral home arrived. They were big, strong men and were able to pick Jessie up and transfer him to a rolling table, the kind with legs that collapsed as soon as you pushed it into an ambulance. Or a hearse.

Since the house was a ranch, they didn't have to worry about steps. If they had, they didn't know what they would have done. They wheeled Jessie out and down the driveway to their black van. They opened the door and lifted him up; the legs collapsed and they pushed him in. With a satisfying *snap*, they closed the door and got into the cab.

Carol pulled the drapes aside and watched from an inside window. The van drove down

the street. After a few seconds, it was out of
view. And just like that, Jessie Giles's life ended.
How was she going to break the news to their
kids?

Later that night, the phone rang at Phyllis
Burke's house. Her forty-five-year-old daughter,
Nancy Billiter, answered it.

"Nancy, its Carol."

"What's wrong? You sound—"

"Nancy, Jessie died."

"Oh, I'm so sorry!"

"It was a heart attack."

Jessie was Nancy's cocaine dealer. That's how
the two women had met. Carol would drop in
at South Boulevard Station on the way home
from work for a drink. South Boulevard Station
was a big restaurant with a friendly bar in
Auburn Hills, another Detroit suburb. Nancy
worked there as a waitress.

The two women just seemed to hit it off.
They had a common interest in mystery novels
and traded paperbacks frequently. Despite their
age difference, they exchanged life stories, the
way drinking buddies do at bars, but they took
it a step further and began socializing.

Nancy was living at her mom's house with
her eight-year-old grandson, Garret; she had
custody of the boy and was hoping to get together enough money to get their own place.
Carol would come over to visit with L'il Man
and Jesseca and they would play with Garret.

Nancy noticed that Jessie Jr. was having

trouble learning how to ride a bike, so she spent hours with the six-year-old, helping him ride a two-wheeler, guiding him up and down the sidewalk in front of her mom's house. Nancy was such a good person.

When Carol told her that the big man had died, she couldn't get there fast enough. She had thought the world of Jessie. Rushing up the steps of Carol's house, she couldn't help but remember how she had helped Jessie and Carol move in barely three months before, and now tragedy had struck.

Carol was bereft. She just didn't know how she could take care of the house and the kids and have a job, all at the same time.

"I'm living with my mom right now," said Nancy. "But maybe I could move in temporarily and help you out. Would you like that?"

Carol's face lit up.

"Oh yes!"

And so, temporarily, Nancy Billiter, a woman who would do anything for a friend, moved in with Carol to help her through her time of grief. One other person moved in, too: Carol's boyfriend, Tim Collier. Carol was the type of woman who needed a man to take care of her. And that's what, she hoped, Tim would do. But Tim had little time for love, at least immediately.

Tim had long planned a California vacation, and shortly after he moved in, he left for the coast. But while he was gone, he called Carol every night. He missed her terribly, and after a week, he cut his vacation short and returned home to live with Carol, her children and Nancy.

Eight

"I think she likes you. I think she, you know, likes you. Romantically."

"No, she doesn't."

"Yes, she does. You can see it in the way she looks at you sometimes. That's it, that's why you're on her side."

"I'm not—"

"You did it together, right?"

Where did Tim get such a crazy idea?

Carol denied she and Nancy were lovers. But Tim was convinced that when he wasn't around, she and Nancy were making love to each other. Carol thought that was crazy.

But Tim had another agenda.

He thought they should do a threesome. He prodded Carol to do it and, finally, she agreed.

"Look, if that'll prove to you that we're straight, okay, I will do it," Carol said.

A few days later, they asked Nancy if she'd be interested in swinging. Nancy wasn't interested. On three different occasions when Tim was high, he tried talking Nancy into swinging with them but to no avail.

Tim was so insistent that Carol finally talked it over with Nancy. Alone. They decided to appease Tim by pretending to go along with his idea. The two women joked about it, calling it their "Chinese scheme."

What they would do is get naked, all three together, and then the women would chicken out. That way, he would get his fantasy, sort of, and he would leave them alone. One night, with the kids sleeping, they decided to try it.

When Nancy and Carol pulled back according to their plan, Tim got really upset and angry. They all started screaming at each other. After Nancy went down to the basement, Carol had to calm him down.

"We don't love each other," Carol insisted.

"Somebody else mentioned that they thought Nancy liked you. Like she was your regular girl-friend," Tim screamed.

"Tim, stop! It's just not true. The closest we got to hugging and kissing each other was, you know, her consoling me at Jessie's funeral. Tim, I love *you.*"

"And I love *you.*"

But he still thought they were having an affair.

They were driving in the car shortly after that when Carol told Tim that Nancy had taken some of her drugs, the stuff usually sold to Jessie's clients, and sold it herself without Carol knowing about it. Carol had discovered the drugs missing and knew to whom the stuff had been sold.

Carol couldn't believe that she did it. She had not said anything to Nancy yet.

"You know, when they steal something small, they are going to steal something big."

"But, Tim, it was just a fifty-dollar rock [of crack]. I don't care. If she had taken the whole thing, yeah, I would be upset, but at the same time, I don't care. I mean, I don't do drugs. It's just, you know, the extra money. I don't care."

Tim cared enough to confront Nancy. She denied taking anything. And when he then confronted Carol and asked her if she was upset that Nancy stole from her, she answered meekly, "Yeah, a little."

It wasn't a strong enough rebuke. Here he was ready to beat the shit out of Nancy for what she'd done and Carol wasn't backing him up. That made him even more furious. Reading his expression, Carol knew what she had done.

The last thing Tim could tolerate was being made to look stupid in front of others; it caused disrespect. This was the second time, the first being when Tim wanted to have sex with the both of them and Carol backed up Nancy about not doing it.

Carol still figured everything would be cool. Tim had moved in; Nancy was helping out. So they had a few problems together, so what?

They'd work it out, and besides, her birthday was coming up.

Carol and Tim started talking about celebrating it with a trip to California. Maybe they could find a house or an apartment in Sacramento and move out there. That didn't sound too bad to Carol. It might be real cool.

Catch some rays, go to some of Tim's old haunts in Sacramento, and look for a place at the same time. A little business, a little pleasure, and maybe a new life at the end of the rainbow.

With the decision made to vacation in California, all that was left was to pack and make sure the kids had child-care. But Carol had one family obligation to take care of before they traveled west.

Carol had promised to visit her dad in Port Huron for Halloween. Jesseca and Jesse wanted to trick-or-treat with their cousin, Lilly, her brother Sam's daughter. Along with her father, they would all be there.

Carol, Tim, Jesseca and L'il Man all piled in the Caddy and tooled on over there. It wasn't too far, maybe thirty miles as the crow flies, but for Carol, it was an extremely emotional trip.

They went to her dad's house in Port Huron. Carol was glad Tim came along, because she was still scared of her father and what she claimed he had done to her. Even today, she wouldn't go to her dad's house unless there was someone else there. Even now, he still touched her and stuff . . . but the kids wanted to trick-or-treat with her brother's daughter.

Tim knew all about the way Carol had been abused. She'd told him awhile back, which was why he didn't say two words to her dad the whole time they were there. And there they were—the incestuous dad, or so Carol said, Dad's girlfriend, Carol's two kids, her brother, his child, and his girlfriend and Carol's boyfriend. They really were one big, happy, dysfunctional family.

They stayed the night of October 31 and went home the next day. They began finalizing the plans for their California vacation. Childcare was all-important to Carol. Since Nancy owed her $200 for coke she'd given her, she offered to forgive the debt if Nancy baby-sat the kids while they were gone.

Nancy didn't have any money to pay off her debt. It was a good offer. Besides, she loved the kids. It was agreed: for eliminating the $200 debt, Nancy would be home to get the two kids up and dressed for school and baby-sit them when they got home. When she went to work at five, she'd take the kids to Nancy's sister Susan's house in Pontiac and Susan would watch them for the three or four hours while Nancy was at work. Nancy would pick them up at nine or ten and get them back home in time for sleep and school the next day.

With the plan set, Carol and Tim left in her green pickup truck for California on November

4. It was Carol's twenty-sixth birthday. They drove across the Rockies and the Great Plains, and inside of three days, they were in Sacramento, where they got a room at a local hotel. Sacramento was a large city, the state's capital, and there were lots of motels and hotels to choose from.

Visiting her dad's had set off a string of painful memories. Carol just had to talk about it. Tim said that he could see how uncomfortable she was.

"Maybe it's just the way my dad is. If we could just hug and touch . . ." Her voice trailed off.

What Tim didn't like was the way her dad was fondling his girlfriend in front of Carol and her brother and all the kids. Tim thought it was "inappropriate to do that in the living room in front of other people."

"I want to kill my dad," she finally said.

How bad did that make her look? Carol wanted to know. How bad was she that she wanted to kill her father?

"Well, just think about it. You know, we could do it and nobody would know," Tim answered.

"What would we do?" she asked.

They could go into her dad's place, Tim continued, and not leave any witnesses. If her brother was there, too bad. Would she be willing to kill her brother and his girlfriend if she was along?

Carol figured that if it occurred during the week, then nobody would be there but her dad.

She didn't think his girlfriend stayed with him. She pointed out that her dad had had several heart attacks and his heart was real bad. He also had some sort of disease in his spine. That led to a discussion about using heroin to kill her father.

Tim liked to cover the angles and he suggested filling up a few syringes. They only needed one to do her dad, but if they got up there and her brother was there with his girlfriend, they needed to be ready. They needed to be prepared: no witnesses.

If the brother was there, he would use his gun and make them lie down on the floor, and Carol could stick him while Tim kept her dad covered. Then it would be her dad's turn.

"Stick one in his balls and one in his eye; so that way, whoever came in and saw this . . . maybe they could put two and two together and see that, you know, to see that he was a molester. Like the killer had left his calling card by killing him in that way," Tim suggested.

Before Carol delivered the death wound, Tim wanted her to tell him, "No more. You won't hurt me no more." Then she would do it and just let him die.

As for the others, her dad's girlfriend, her brother and his girlfriend, they could give them overdoses of heroin and then make it look like a robbery. Her dad had guns and money and other stuff in his house that someone would want to steal. They would also leave the needles at the scene.

After discussing it, they decided to "do" her dad when they got back. But then she realized that they were broke. They couldn't kill him the way they wanted without the heroin and they couldn't buy the heroin without the money. Still, Carol liked the plan.

Maybe if they got some money and got the heroin . . . but guilt began to eat away at her. She agreed to do it, but at the same time, she kept the thought in her mind that it wasn't going to happen. She kept telling herself that everything would turn out all right.

On Saturday, November 8, Carol and Tim were still in Sacramento when Carol called Nancy to see how things were. It was 8:00 P.M. on the West Coast; 11:00 P.M. in Michigan. During that conversation, Nancy told her about the burglary.

Someone had broken in through the kitchen and stolen jewelry from the house. Nancy was so scared, she didn't leave until the sun came up. Then she had to go to work.

"Well, Nancy, who do you think did it?" Carol asked.

"Maybe your stepdaughter Stephanie."

Stephanie Johnson was Jessie's daughter from a first marriage.

"We had a conversation and we got into it," Nancy continued. "Steph was upset that you went to California and didn't tell anybody about it."

This argument made Nancy think that Steph was the one who broke into the house because she was the only one who knew what time Nancy would be gone and how long she'd be gone.

"I'll take care of it when I get home," Carol answered, clearly exasperated and not a little worried that her home, and that of her children, had some sort of security breach. "I'll find out who did it when I get home," she promised.

Carol hung up and told Tim what Nancy had said about the break-in. Tim got visibly quiet and withdrawn. He didn't want to talk to her. She hated when there was so much silence and distance between them.

"What's the matter Tim?" Carol finally asked.

"I think Nancy did it. Why would Steph steal the stuff? Because whatever Steph had wanted, after Jessie died, you gave it to her."

And why would she come into the house and just steal the jewelry and not the fifty-five-inch TV and VCR in the bedroom? Tim wondered. He figured the answer was whoever burglarized the place took stuff that could be sold fast on the street for drugs. Or money to buy drugs.

Nancy had a coke habit she needed to support; Steph didn't. Nancy couldn't support her habit just by waitressing, Tim figured. She owed Carol for drugs she'd given her before they left, and Nancy had had to pay off the debt by baby-sitting the kids while they were gone.

Tim was convinced Nancy took the stuff and faked the burglary. She took it to sell fast and to buy drugs.

"We gotta get her," Tim said.

Carol, though, wasn't so sure it was Nancy. How could they know for sure who had done it—the house being back in Michigan and them being here in California? They didn't talk about it anymore that night. But the next morning, they were both aggravated enough about their privacy being invaded by person or persons unknown that they decided to return to Michigan.

They had driven west in Carol's truck. As they climbed the Rockies, they discovered it had bad brakes. They didn't want to take the time to nurse it cross-country or spend the money on a brake job. Carol called Greyhound and got the schedule and location of the bus station. On Sunday night, they abandoned the truck and picked up the bus home.

While they sprawled in adjoining seats, the bus made its way through Green River, Utah, in country that had once belonged to Butch Cassidy and the Sundance Kid. Some legends said that Cassidy had made it back from Bolivia and was buried somewhere nearby in a secret grave.

The bus passed through Glenwood Springs, Colorado, where Doc Holliday was buried in a cemetery up on a hill, his gravestone marked with a poker hand of aces and eights, the dead man's hand. The town was now a preferred retirement site for senior citizens from the east.

They traveled out on the Kansas prairie that Wyatt Earp and Bat Masterson had once roamed. Like zombies moving through the pale yellow light of the bus stations, Carol and Tim sleepily switched buses a few times along the route. It was always night, it seemed, and the cafeterias served the same tasteless food. Except for the chili, which was always good.

Mile after mile, they chattered on about this or that, but they never talked about the break-in, Carol recalled. To her, anyway, it was no big deal. After all, only material things had been taken. Who cared about those?

They had told no one they were coming home and so it was a surprised Nancy Billiter who looked up on the cold afternoon of November 12 to see the key turning in the door and her friend Carol and Carol's boyfriend, Tim, come marching in with their suitcases.

Nancy, still surprised, asked how the trip was. Carol said it was fine.

"Why are you back so soon?" Nancy asked suspiciously.

Carol and Tim ignored that question. Nancy must have been thinking it had something to do with the burglary, but she didn't let on.

Carol made a careful walk through the house to see if anything else had been stolen. She walked upstairs with her bags and looked in the closet and saw that the safe was gone, as were the VCR and the TV. There was something else in the closet that was missing, but she couldn't pinpoint exactly what it was.

It had been a long bus ride. Tim went into the bathroom to relieve himself. Through the closed door, Carol told him that something in the closet was missing, but she couldn't figure out what it was.

Nancy was suddenly by her side.

"Come talk to me," said the older woman.

The two friends went down to the living room and sat on the sofa, where Nancy peppered her with questions about the trip. Where did they go? What did they see? They blathered on for a while and then when Tim came out of the bathroom, he and Carol went out to the garage to get the gold Caddy. Carol went to put something in the trunk—she couldn't remember what—and that's when she saw it.

"It's the kid's piggy bank!"

Now, Carol knew for sure that Nancy was the burglar and not someone else, because she didn't tell her that the piggy bank was stolen and yet she found it in the very car Nancy had been using to drive to work while they were gone. Tim and Carol theorized that Nancy had stolen the goods, pawned them for drugs, and then made it look like someone else had broken into the house.

"Leave the bank there for now," Tim ordered.

Carol went out back and looked at the kitchen door, the one Nancy said the burglar broke to get in. There was one big hole, boarded up. Nobody but a midget could have climbed through that. And anybody who did climb through would have gotten cut.

Nancy never mentioned anything about blood on the kitchen floor.

"Why don't we see if we can find the stuff that was stolen," Tim suggested.

They took the Caddy and traveled around town to three different pawnshops, trying to find the jewelry that had been stolen. Carol knew that if the stuff had been pawned, there would be a name on the pawn ticket.

No dice. The pawnshops were a dead end.

They got back home at about 2:45 P.M It was still the same day, November 12. They agreed to let Nancy continue using the car to go to work. Then, when she got home, they would check the trunk. If she got rid of the piggy bank, they would know for sure.

"What do you want to do now?" Carol asked

"I'm going into Detroit to get some drugs," Tim replied.

When the kids got back an hour later, they were surprised and delighted to see their mother home. Nancy, meanwhile, changed into her work uniform, and Carol volunteered to drive her to work.

* * *

In the interview room, Messina leaned back in his chair.

That didn't make sense, Messina thought. That just didn't make sense. As Carol continued to talk, he tried to figure it out.

They were going to let Nancy take the car to see if she got rid of the piggy bank. If she did, that would prove her guilt. Instead, Carol had inexplicably deviated from their plan?

Why? Unless, there never was a plan and she was making that part of her statement up.

"Anyway, when I got home after dropping Nancy off at work, I opened the trunk and took the piggy bank inside," Carol continued.

By 6:30 P.M., Tim still wasn't back. Everyone was hungry, so they left Tim a note saying they were going down to the Ram's Horn for dinner. They had a nice dinner and returned by 7:30 P.M. Tim still wasn't back.

The bus ride, and the tension of the break-in, had made Carol very tired; she told the kids to be quiet for a half hour and she took a nap. While she lay on her bed upstairs, she could hear the kids watching TV downstairs in the living room.

She didn't realize that a half hour had turned into two hours until Tim woke her at 9:30 P.M. She got up quickly and put the kids to bed. By ten o'clock, they were tucked in. Carol went into her bedroom where Tim was seated on the bed.

From the front of his belt, he pulled a revolver that he liked to carry. He said that when he was in Detroit, he had to prove himself.

"Reload it," Tim ordered.

Apparently, he had shot someone. Carol didn't ask any questions; she knew better.

From a shelf in the closet, Carol took down a box of shells. She pressed the release on the side of the automatic and the clip popped down. It was empty. Unless he had fired some of the bullets at another time, he must have fired them in Detroit.

She reloaded the weapon—there was space for eight bullets, she said—and pushed the clip back into the stock. Then she handed it over to Tim, who put it away. Later, a little bit after 11:00 P.M., Carol was washing the dishes in the kitchen when Bill, a friend of Nancy's, drove the waitress home and dropped her off. After coming in, she asked Carol:

"You got any drugs?"

"No," Carol replied.

Just then, Tim walked into the kitchen.

"I do," he said brightly.

Carol didn't want her kids waking up to see them smoking and insisted they go downstairs. So they all went downstairs into the basement. It was furnished with a few sofas, tables and an extra bed that Carol immediately went to lounge on.

Nancy had an abnormal fear of spiders. She

was afraid spiders would crawl on her if she slept in the bed in the basement. Instead, she slept upstairs on an uncomfortable couch. Carol thought her fear was silly, especially since she sacrificed her comfort for it. Nancy, though, had no problems sitting on the bed when others were there.

Nancy loaded up her crack pipe and came over to sit at the foot of the bed, where she began smoking. Tim sat on a chair in front of her with his elbows back, lounging. Carol pulled out a cigarette from a pack and lit up. Periodically she took a swig from a one-liter Pepsi she had brought down with her.

The conversation went back and forth breezily, about California and about Nancy's work, until Carol asked Tim what time it was. He looked at his watch.

"One o'clock," he answered.

Nancy made a phone call about 1:20 A.M. to see if her friend Bill, who had dropped her off, had made it home safely. He had and she felt relieved. Carol put the phone on the bed so she could see it ring, because the ringer was broken but an incoming call would light up the dial.

"So, Nancy, tell me about the break-in again," Tim asked.

He wanted to know how she knew where the safe was.

"What safe? Tim, I didn't break into the

house; I wouldn't, you know. I wouldn't steal anything from Carol."

Carol explained that the stuff that was stolen was her deceased husband's jewelry.

"It's wrong to steal from a dead man," Carol said.

Nancy readily agreed.

"I think you're lying," Tim said, looking her dead in the eye. "I think you know where the stuff is. What do you think, Carol?"

Carol told her erstwhile "friend" that she thought she had done it, because ". . . I found the bank." And then Carol picked up the bank to show her that it wasn't in the trunk of the car anymore.

Nancy hastily explained that she had found it at the end of the driveway and put it in the trunk of the car. But Tim was tired of the bull-shit.

"I think you're lying," Tim said quietly.

Carol thought Tim had left his gun upstairs, which was why she was surprised when he flashed across the room and pointed the muzzle of the automatic close to Nancy's face. If Tim twitched, Nancy was hamburger.

Nancy didn't take him seriously.

"Stop playing," she said.

Tim swung. Cold steel bit into soft flesh. At that same moment, Carol heard a noise from upstairs. Fearful the kids were up, Carol ran up the stairs, glancing back long enough to see blood seeping from Nancy's face.

After checking on the kids—they were all right, still asleep—Carol went to go back down. Descending the steps, she heard moaning coming from the basement.

When she got back, she saw Nancy sprawled on the bed, spread-eagled. Her wrists were tied to the bed frame with pantyhose. Nancy still had her uniform on from work, but she had one leg out of her pants.

Carol couldn't figure that one out: how had her leg gotten out of her pants? And she wasn't wearing any panties or pantyhose. Looking closer, she saw that the pantyhose binding her wrists to the bed were one color and the pair binding her legs was another. Then there was the washcloth.

Tim had stuffed it in her mouth to stop her from screaming. The gag was secured with another pair of hose tied around her head.

Tim hit Nancy in the stomach. He hit her again and again and again, his rage crashing down like a pile driver into her saggy middle.

Nancy kept moaning.

"Shut up, shut up," Tim yelled, hitting her harder and harder. "If you don't, I'll kill ya right here in the basement."

Carol heard Nancy making noises; that's how she knew she was conscious. Then Tim pointed the gun at Nancy. He handed Carol a syringe and said, "Shoot her."

Carol looked at it. She had no idea what it was loaded with, but she knew it was full. Tim ordered her to inject Nancy with the mystery liquid. But Carol didn't want to. Hell, she had no idea what was in the syringe. She tried to stall, but Tim insisted.

Carol looked down the barrel of the gun. She was convinced that if she didn't do it, he would kill her. So she did, sticking the needle in Nancy's ankle. Carefully, quickly, she pushed the plunger and watched the fluid drain into her leg. Nancy moaned.

Tim hit her in the face again and ordered her to shut up.

"Okay," said Carol, standing up, "it's done. I injected her."

"Fill it up again," Tim ordered in a cold voice.

He pointed at the shelf near the foot of the bed. For the first time since they'd come downstairs, Carol saw the clear plastic jug filled with hydrochloric acid Tim had placed there. She knew what the stuff was. Jessie had used it to fill up the lawn mower's battery.

Tim had decided to kill Nancy by injecting her with the deadly acid.

With no choice, Carol plunged the needle into the jug and pulled the plunger back. She tried taking her time filling it up, but he kept hurrying her. She explained that she had to make sure she got the air out of it—otherwise, Nancy would die from an embolism.

The clear white fluid filled up the hollow cylinder to the halfway point. She brought it up to the light and squeezed a bit out of the tip. Carol's fright-filled eyes followed the path of the needle toward Nancy's arm. It was like somebody else doing it. Finally, when she could delay no longer, Carol delivered the injection into Nancy's arm and watched as the sharp needle penetrated the skin and the acid burned her.

"I saw that," Tim said.

He'd been watching her like a hawk.

"You only had it half full. Fill it up. All the way."

Carol couldn't bluff anymore. She had to fill the syringe to the top, or Tim would kill her for not doing what he wanted. She went through the same procedure, going slower, trying to think.

When she could delay no longer, she shot the liquid subcutaneously, hoping it wouldn't get into any veins or do anything too damaging. But despite her best efforts, Nancy moaned in pain.

Tim watched with a relentless eye, smoking intensely, covering both of them with the automatic. Whenever Nancy moaned, he ordered her to be quiet.

Six times, Tim told her to inject Nancy; six times, Carol filled the syringe with the hydrochloric acid and plunged the needle into Nancy's skin. Carol gave injections in Nancy's leg, arm and stomach; then Tim told her, "The neck"; and she plunged the needle into her neck.

Nancy kept moaning and moaning. Then, suddenly, the moaning stopped. Her eyes stayed open, but there was nothing there; the light had gone out.

Nancy Billiter was dead. Just as well. By that time, the needle was spent.

Suddenly, Nancy jerked up. She hadn't been dead after all. Maybe she was playing possum or maybe she had just gone out for a minute. Whatever. She rose up and began struggling against her bonds.

Tim whacked at her face with the barrel of the gun. The metal slammed into flesh. She bled heavily, but the force of the blow drove her back down to the mattress.

"Lay down and be quiet," Tim commanded.

Carol thought she heard her kids waking up and ran upstairs to check on them. They were fine. When she came down again, Tim was back to punching Nancy in the stomach. Carol stood by the foot of the bed. When he moved back, Carol stared at Nancy in horror.

Nancy's skin was exposed. Her blouse was open. There was extensive bluish and yellowish bruising around her midsection, like she'd just spent an hour with Muhammad Ali pounding her gut.

Tim told Carol to get a wet towel. She wasn't sure why she was doing this, but she wouldn't dare ask Tim—not now, not when he was so mad. She figured to herself that maybe Nancy's face was so bloody, she was to wipe it off.

Carol wrung it out and handed it to Tim. He went over to the laundry machine and poured bleach on it. He used the bleach-soaked cloth to wipe off Nancy's blood that had spattered the wall. Then he wiped his hands with the towel. When she heard another noise from upstairs, Carol left to check on the kids again. She came back down a few minutes later. That's when she saw Tim holding the towel over Nancy's face.

Tim was smothering her.

Gasping for air, Nancy squirmed and kicked; then, suddenly, she wasn't fighting any longer. She just lay there, limp. Hesitantly, Carol came closer and sat on the bed next to her friend. Tim got up and walked away, leaving the towel over her face.

Carol thought she could hear her breathing. Maybe she was still alive. Carol pulled the towel down and freed up her air and sinus passages. Carol heard noise again from upstairs. Her kids. She looked at her watch. It was six o'clock. She had to get them up at seven in time for school.

Leaving Nancy the way she was, they left the basement and went upstairs together. Behind them, they closed the basement door and put a knife in the jamb so the kids couldn't get in; the door didn't have a regular lock.

Nine

Tim wondered what it would be like to have sex with a dead body. Carol thought that was repugnant and told him so. Instead, Tim seemed to be satiated when they rutted like pigs on the sofa.

Afterward, Carol looked at her watch. It was 6:00 A.M., November 13.

Tim gazed through the blinds. He was convinced that the phone call Nancy made had not been to the guy who dropped her off but to the cops, who were now staking the house out waiting for them. Carol figured his paranoia came from the stuff he kept smoking.

She tried to reason with him. It was the crack talking, not him. Tim's response?

He was across the room in a flash and pulled Carol to the door, opened it and, still holding her arm, pulled her down the long driveway to see if there was a police car at the curb.

"Tim, there's nothing," Carol urged.

Tim kept looking, at the curb, across the street at the church, at the parking lot next door. There was nothing, save another dreary

November morning beginning with a gray overcast sky and a sharp chill in the air.

Before they got to the curb, Tim ordered,
"Go back in the house."

Carol went back in and started to walk toward
the bedroom. She planned on calling 911 because Nancy was still breathing when they left
her, and Carol was concerned. She figured that
if she dialed 911 but said nothing into the receiver, instead leaving it off the hook, they
would trace the call. But then Tim came in
from outside, so she couldn't reach the bedroom; he'd be suspicious if she went in alone.
Instead, she went to the bathroom.

When she came out, he went into their bedroom and was gazing intently out the window.
He still thought the cops were out there. Then
he turned and quickly ran into the kids' rooms.
Anxious, lest he do something insane, Carol
followed him.

Tim did the same thing; he looked out L'il
Man's window, then Jesseca's, surprised there
were no cops. Then it was into the bathroom
and looking out the bathroom window and
closing the shower curtain so no one from outside could look in. He went back out to the
kitchen and he looked out the dining room
window and the kitchen window again. Finally
he went downstairs to the basement.

He was down there only a few seconds, but
he heard the floorboards above him creaking,
so he shot up the stairs to find Carol walking

toward the bedroom. His eyes tracked her as she got the kids up and quickly dressed them for school.

"Mama, I don't want to go to school. I'm sick," complained her daughter.

No way would Carol let her child stay home, not with Nancy trussed up like a turkey in the basement, and Lord knew if she was still breathing.

Carol insisted: her daughter had to go to school. Jesseca wasn't very happy, but she acquiesced. She knew her mom always acted in her best interests.

Carol saw both of them off and onto the bus. She went back inside.

"We have to get rid of her," Tim said. "We have to get rid of Nancy."

Carol remembered Nancy's bloody face and shivered at the thought. No matter how she'd tried to help her, someplace, deep down, she knew now that she was dead.

"And then there's the blood on the mattress, so we have to get rid of the mattress, too," Tim added.

Carol was afraid she would show her fear, that her voice would crack. She didn't want to show him she was scared. The whole time they had been talking, he had been walking around the house, looking out the windows, and somehow he had gotten the gun in his hand. She was afraid anything would set him off, anything, especially her fear of discovery.

"How can we just get rid of her?" she said out loud.

"Well, I can take her to Rouge Park or someplace in Detroit. Just leave her in the park or wherever."

"Well, you can't do that in daylight."

"Then we'll have to wait for tonight," Tim said.

He mumbled something about making Nancy look like the victim of a drug deal gone bad. Tim pulled the knife out of the door to the basement. Carol followed him downstairs, where he immediately checked to make sure that no one had come through the basement windows.

Carol looked over at the bloody, unmoving heap on the bed. She didn't dare step closer, for fear she would find out for sure that Nancy was dead. By staying back, there was still a small sliver of hope.

They went back upstairs and Tim said, "Come on, let's go."

"Where to?" asked Carol, putting her coat on.

Tim wanted to go to Flint to get a pickup truck. The idea he had was to use the truck to transport the body to a place where they could dump it.

On the way, Tim explained that they were in this together. Carol didn't reply.

Tim said if they got caught, the cops would use one against the other. They needed to stay strong. But if they got arrested, for whatever reason, "just look in their eyes and don't act fidgety. Because that's what they look for. If you use your hands or you move your legs when you talk, they know you're lying."

Carol talked with her hands. It made Carol more nervous to sit motionless.

"If you look in their eyes and ya tell them, they'll believe you," Tim stated.

Carol didn't think she could do it; Tim though, seemed able to do it. He could lie to someone by looking him or her right in the eye and be totally convincing. Tim always talked about cops like they used this psychology to get you to confess and to do what they wanted you to do. And then Tim said what he'd been saying since the day that she met him back at the hospital:

"You never leave witnesses to a crime."

Carol did her best to look him in the eye and not look scared.

When they got to Flint, they drove up and down unfamiliar streets, at least unfamiliar to Carol, but Tim seemed to know where he was going. Tim was looking for a friend's place. He had a friend who had a garage. After a while, they found the place and they went in to talk to somebody.

"Know where I can get a truck?" Tim asked his friend.

His friend told him to come back in an hour.

They got back in the car and went over to Tim's uncle Sammy's house.

The man who answered the door was in his early fifties, tall and thin. She didn't know him, but from what Tim had said about him in the past, it sounded like Sammy was his dad's brother. The two greeted each other warmly and then Sammy invited them in.

Tim and his uncle smoked crack while Carol watched. She didn't say a word. Finally, Tim had had enough and said, "Come on, let's go."

They went back to his friend's place to pick up the truck, but the guy had punked out. He couldn't get them a truck. By then, Carol was starting to get worried about her kids. They'd be getting home, she wouldn't be there, they'd start looking for her, and they'd open the door to the basement. Whoops! "Hey, Ma, what's Aunt Nancy doin' with all that blood over her face, and her dead and everything?"

That was the last thing Carol wanted to happen. But Tim rode around Flint for a while anyway, until Carol told him they had to get back to the house.

"Nancy's back there," she reminded him.

They had a body they had to get rid of.

Tim turned the car around and headed for the interstate, got on and began clocking at about 70 mph.

They hadn't been gone as long as Carol thought; they got home around 1:30 P.M. It was still early. First thing Tim did was state that they had to "get rid of Nancy and the bed." They went down to the basement.

Nothing had changed. Nancy was still tied up to the bed. Nancy's face was still bloody. Nancy was still dead. Carol noticed that the dead woman's hands were an unnatural shade of white.

Tim got a pair of scissors and severed the bonds around her hands and feet. The pantyhose were still tied to the bed but not to her. The hose wouldn't be able to be used as a clue when the cops eventually found her, Tim figured.

"Come on, help me," Tim ordered.

Tim wrapped her up in the blanket and then Carol grabbed her by the head and they started to pull her up the stairs. Tim walked up backward first, carrying her legs; Carol followed in the back, holding up her head.

Maybe it was the way Carol was holding the blanket. She wasn't sure. Whatever it was, the damn thing ripped. Nancy's head fell out and hit the floor with a loud *thud*. She didn't moan. If there had been any doubt before, there was none now.

Nancy Billiter was definitely dead.

Carol felt bad; she'd dropped her dead friend's head. She picked her up again. Tim was pulling her, and Carol was barely able to keep Nancy's head above the ground. But they got her up the steps and then, when they got up the basement steps, they walked a little bit into the kitchen, then down the breezeway steps. It was only three steps. Tim walked too fast down them and Carol dropped the blanket and Nancy's head hit the ground again.

Tim finished the job himself, pulling the corpse into the garage. Carol's car was parked backward in the garage. He took her around the middle and set her down.

"Help me put her in."

Carol came over. Tim went around to the driver's side of the door and popped open the trunk. Carol helped lift her, this time taking the feet. She was very heavy. Carol's arms and shoulders burned with the effort. She started to feel weak. Tim saw her struggling; he came over before she dropped her, and grabbed the blanket, and sat her up in the trunk.

She was too big. He tried to bend her, but she wouldn't go; rigor mortis had made her stiff as a board. He laid her down toward the left side and managed with great effort to get her in sideways. The blanket at the top parted.

Carol saw Nancy's face, a blue-white death mask laced with bright red blood, which was stuck in her hair like some thick syrup. She wanted to look away, but something just made her continue to stare.

Tim closed the trunk on her and went around to drive when Carol spied Nancy's shoe. It had fallen to the ground when Tim pushed her in. She picked it up and gave it to Tim, who nonchalantly popped the trunk again and tossed it in.

It was 1:30 in the afternoon. Carol knew the kids would be home at 3:20 P.M. That gave them a little under two hours to get rid of her and get back. But they also had to get rid of the mattress and they didn't have a truck.

They thought about that—the mattress was too big to fit in the car. The mattress with all of Nancy's blood on it. What could they do with it? Tim decided to bleach it and hide it in the garage.

He went back to the basement. Carol gave him a few minutes, then followed. When she got there, Tim had already treated the mattress with the bleach. She didn't smell anything, but she assumed that he had done it, since it was his idea.

They carried the mattress together up the stairs and out into the garage. Tim climbed on her car and up into the garage's attic, not really an attic but the four-by-fours and two-by-fours that laced through the top of the garage right below the ceiling.

He pushed the mattress up into the latticework. When he was satisfied it was lying there okay, he stepped back down on the car's roof and down to the garage floor.

They went back downstairs again and got the two small box springs the mattress had lain on. They brought those up and put them up in the rafters in a different section of the garage. Everything was secreted in such a way that when the garage doors were opened, you wouldn't see the mattresses and springs, at least not immediately.

"You can lie about the blood on the mattress," Tim said, sounding out of breath, "but if the police, ya know, come over there, they'll test it and see it's Nancy's blood. I have to find a truck so I can get rid of them, but until then, we'll just leave it here."

Back in the basement, Carol swept the area where the bed had been. Tim cut the pantyhose off the frame and put it in a garbage bag. Then he took the bed frame apart. When he was finished, he put the frame away in a corner.

"Change your clothes," Tim ordered.

She put the old clothes in the garbage bag and put the garbage bag in the kitchen next to the garbage can. With their work done, they decided to wait for dark before disposing of the body.

Soon the kids came home from school. They were hungry, so Carol fixed them each a sandwich. Then she sat down to do homework with them, and afterward, they watched a little TV.

Tim, meanwhile, was going from room to room. When he was out of sight, he'd take a hit of crack, pacing from room to room, looking out the window; he was still worrying the cops were there. Gradually the day wore down; the light faded; until finally, it was dark.

Carol fell asleep.

* * *

November 13, 1997

It was 8:30 P.M. Tim woke her. She had been sleeping for hours. During that time, he had gone back to Flint to scout out a dumping location and had come back.

Carol got up and ate part of a sandwich. Then she helped the kids get ready for bed. Jesseca had a headache, so she gave her some Tylenol to help her sleep. Her son didn't want to go to sleep because he'd had a nap earlier. It took a while to put him down. By the time they were both tucked in and sleeping, it was a little after nine.

The stress was killing her. Carol took another nap and Tim woke her at midnight. Time to finish it.

With both kids sleeping soundly, but without a baby-sitter in case they awakened, Carol and Tim got into the gold Caddy and drove out of the driveway of the home, past the police station, on the way to the interstate.

As snow fell, the wipers whisked back and forth. Behind the wheel, Carol peered out into the darkness. Tim thought she was driving too slowly and insisted on driving. Carol pulled off into a snowbank, where they switched seats. Tim took over. He looked at the illuminated dashboard. The fuel tank arrow was on EMPTY.

"We need gas," he said.

They really shouldn't have stopped. After all, they had a body in the trunk! But if they didn't, they'd get stuck someplace between West Bloomfield and Pontiac. Sure, it was cold, but that didn't mean the body wouldn't start to stink. And that's all they needed; a suspicious tow truck operator reporting a strange odor in their car to the cops.

Tim found a station that was open and quickly filled the tank. He also filled a big red five-gallon gas can that he had happened to bring along. It was the kind of can you could buy in any auto supply store.

They got on Interstate 70 and headed north into the driving snow. An hour later, they got off at the Flint exit. They had to stop by some railroad tracks to let a train pass. Tim wouldn't wait; he got out of line instead of waiting. After they turned around, two white guys in the truck behind them rolled down their windows and shouted out an epithet. Tim reached for the gun in his waistband.

"Let me shoot them motherfuckers," Tim hissed. "Let me shoot them; let me shoot them."

"No, fuck! I'm not gonna let you," Carol shouted back. "I'm not gonna let you shoot them."

Tim's automatic wasn't the only gun in the car. Carol carried a .32 automatic hidden between the two front seats.

"C'mon, let's shoot them."

"For what?"

It was like Tim always wanted to do something like that. He always wanted to shoot everybody, anybody that bothered him. Maybe he thought he'd be bigger in her eyes if she saw him do it.

Carol told him they didn't have time, but Tim insisted.

"Leave them alone," Carol said firmly.

Tim went around the block like he was going back to get them. Carol realized that if she said yes, he'd do it. Instead, Carol insisted that they must dump the body; she wanted to be done with the killing. That's when Tim pulled into the park.

Carol had no idea where they were, just that it was dark and silent. Suddenly the two white guys that had dissed Tim were long gone, distant encumbrances that had been shown mercy.

Tim backed into the park's lot, so the back of the car faced the river. When they got out, he grabbed the gas can, walked a few paces down the snow-covered path. He stopped, looked around.

"Okay, right here."

"Well, what are we gonna do?"

The idea, he said, was to bring Nancy to this spot and burn her. Nobody would see because it was a secluded spot.

"Let's get it over with," she said.

Carol thrust her frozen hands into her pockets. The snow was coming down heavier. Their breaths were heavy white plumes.

They went back to the car. Tim looked around to make sure no other cars were coming. Satisfied at their isolation, he popped the trunk. Looking around again, Tim sat Nancy up and grabbed her like he was hugging her. He pulled her out and onto the ground.

Carol started to grab Nancy's feet and he just pulled her out, going with the momentum of the body, slinging her over his shoulder. She closed the trunk and followed Tim up the path.

Carol tripped over something and fell. She got back up and by the time she caught up, her boyfriend had dropped the trussed-up body to the ground and was dousing it with gasoline. The awful smell permeated the blanket and came up and hit her nostrils with a sickeningly sweet stench. Carol kept guard, looking around, making sure no one was coming.

"When I tell you, go back and start the car and be ready to go," Tim ordered as he continued to pour.

A car came down the street.

"Get down," Tim ordered.

Carol hid behind a tree. When the car was gone, Tim poured out the remaining gasoline. Carol saw him leave a small trail of twigs and leaves leading up to the gasoline-drenched body. It was really a fuse that he intended to light. It would burn along the ground and when it hit the body, *poof!* It would go up in flames, destroying the evidence.

"Okay, start the car," Tim ordered.

"Well, you got the keys."

He stood there for a minute, thinking. Then, instead of giving her the keys, he gave her a lighter.

"You're gonna light her. Light the gas," he said.

Carol hadn't bargained for that. She didn't know what they were doing. What did she know about disposing of a body by burning it? But this wasn't the time to disagree with Tim.

Tim put the gas can in the trunk. Then he went and got into the car and told her that when he gave the signal, "light it."

Carol looked around. She was scared; she didn't know what to do. Tim cracked the door open and peered out. No one was coming.

"Light it," he ordered.

She looked down at about a five-foot trail of leaves and twigs, saturated with gas that led toward the body. Carol took a piece of paper out of her pocket, lit it, and put it down on the ground. But it didn't hit the gas. When the paper went out, she bent down and lit the gas. When it caught fire, she ran to the car.

She looked back. It was a small, weak fire. Tim pulled out and onto the street and hit the accelerator. Never mind it was snowing and icy. He wanted to get the hell out of there.

"Did the body catch fire?" Tim asked.

Carol said she didn't know. Tim was upset, real upset that she hadn't lit the body. He repeated that that was what she was supposed to do, to make sure the body was lit. That way, she'd burn and nobody'd recognize her.

"I lit the trail close to the body," she lied. "It should catch."

There was no more time to waste. Tim drove around some streets that were foreign to her, until he pulled up in front of Uncle Sammy's house. They knocked on the door. Carol hadn't seen Tim pull the gas can out of the car, but there it was, in his hand. He was putting it down on the steps inside the house after Uncle Sammy let them in. They went upstairs, into the living room. Two of Sammy's girlfriends were already there enjoying his hospitality.

Tim pulled some crack out of his pocket. He gave Sammy some and the two girls some. The four of them lit up and smoked, drifting to heaven on the high, not worrying about anything except where the next pipe was coming from.

He started socializing, like they had just come over for a Sunday dinner. *What's your name? Where you from? Was her brother so-and-so? Yada yada yada.* After a while, Tim got bored.

"Let's go," he said, and they were back in the car driving through snowdrifts. "I want to see if the body burned," he said, and they drove to the park.

There were no flames, no fire, and no parked

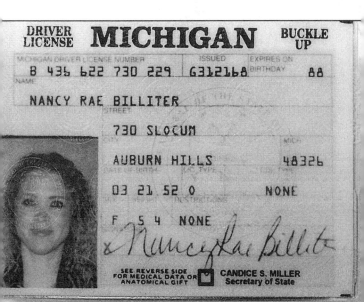

Driver's license photograph of victim, Nancy Billiter.

Billiter's body was wrapped in a blanket by the murderers and then dumped in a snowy field outside Flint, Michigan where they attempted to burn it.

Police found tire tracks near the crime scene.

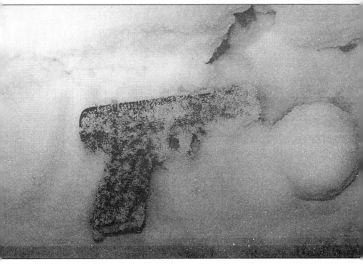

The gun used to kill Billiter as found near the body dump site.

Billiter's body as seen
by police when they
first discovered it.

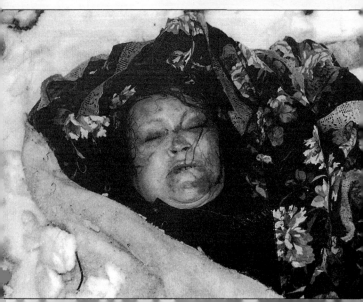

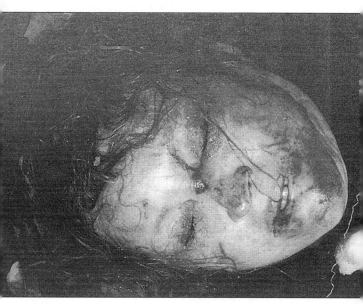

Her face was covered with blood and badly beaten.

"South Boulevard Station," the name of the bar where
Billiter worked as a waitress, was printed on her
T-shirt and led investigators to discover her identity.

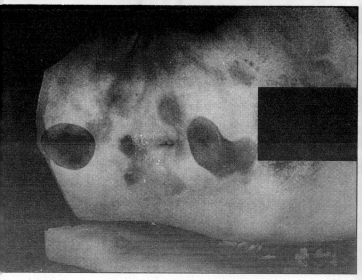

Bruises and mottled blood covered Billiter's body.

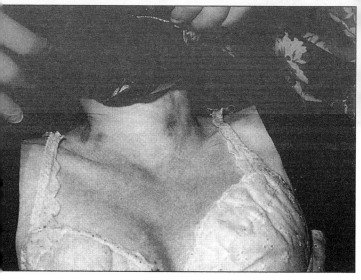

Bruises on Billiter's neck caused by multiple injections.

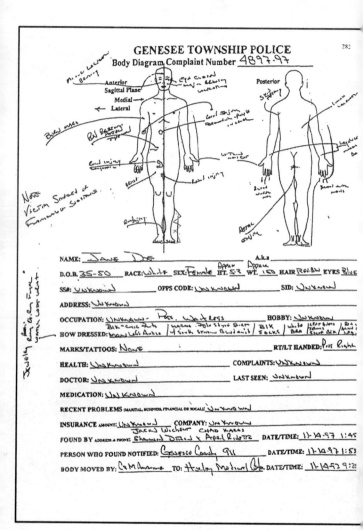

The coroner's diagram of Billiter's corpse shortly after
police discovered her.

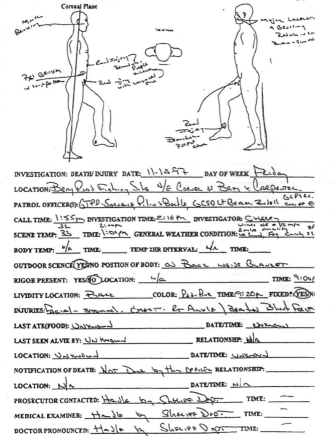

Coronal Plane

INVESTIGATION: DEATH/ INJURY DATE: 11-14-97 DAY OF WEEK: Friday

LOCATION: Bear Pond Fishing Site N/E Corner of Bear & Carpenter

PATROL OFFICER(S): GTPD-Source, Pilon & Bartle, GCSO Lt Bean, Zudell chief of E GCPLEC

CALL TIME: 1:55pm INVESTIGATION TIME: 2:16 PM INVESTIGATOR: Curry

SCENE TEMP: 33 / 32 TIME: 1:04pm / 2:00pm GENERAL WEATHER CONDITION: Winds NE @ 12 m/h, 2 mile visibility, Ice & mud, Fog, Cloudy 29°

BODY TEMP: N/A TIME: _____ TEMP 2HR INTERVAL: N/A TIME: _____

OUTDOOR SCENCE YES/NO POSTION OF BODY: on Back inside Blanket

RIGOR PRESENT: YES/NO LOCATION: N/A TIME: 9:00f

LIVIDITY LOCATION: Back COLOR: Red-Pink TIME: 9:20A FIXED: YES/NO

INJURIES: Facial - Stomach. Chest. Rt Ankle / Beaten Blunt Force

LAST ATE(FOOD): Unknown DATE/TIME: Unknown

LAST SEEN ALVIE BY: Unknown RELATIONSHIP: N/A

LOCATION: Unknown DATE/TIME: Unknown

NOTIFICATION OF DEATH: Not Done by this Officer RELATIONSHIP: _____

LOCATION: N/A DATE/TIME: N/A

PROSECUTOR CONTACTED: Handle by Sheriff Dept. TIME: _____

MEDICAL EXAMINER: Handle by Sheriff Dept. TIME: _____

DOCTOR PRONOUNCED: Handle by Sheriff Dept. TIME: _____

GILES
CAROL   LYNN
DOB: 11 / 04 / 71
RACE: WHITE
SEX: FEMALE
HEIGHT: 510
WEIGHT: 125
EYE COLOR: BROWN
HAIR COLOR: BROWN
COMP#: 19738
PHOTO#: 102275
CHARGE: 0101 MURDER FIREARM

Carol Giles's mug shot after her arrest.

COLLIER
TIMMY   ORLANDO
DOB: 02 / 05 / 69
RACE: BLACK
SEX: MALE
HEIGHT: 506
WEIGHT: 140
EYE COLOR: BROWN
HAIR COLOR: BLACK
COMP#: 19738
PHOTO#: 102271
CHARGE: 0101 MURDER FIREARM

Tim Collier's mug shot after his arrest.

The home the Giles family was renting at the time of the murder. (*Author's collection*)

Billiter claimed that a burglar had broken into the rear entrance of the Giles's home and had stolen some valuable items, a claim that angered Collier.

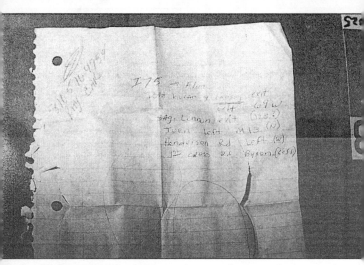

Directions to the area in Flint, Michigan, where Carol
Giles and Tim Collier dumped Nancy Billiter's body.
This note was confiscated during a search of
the suspects' home.

The mattress on which Nancy Billiter was murdered.
It was recovered from the garage rafters in the
Giles's home.

A search of the "murder" house turned up a carton of bullets for the gun Collier carried.

The holster Collier used to carry his gun in.

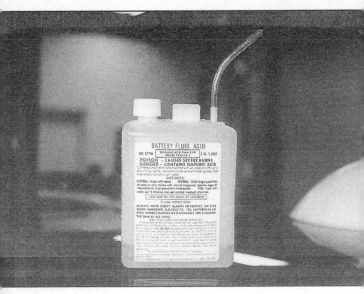

Battery acid from this bottle was injected into
Nancy Billiter's body.

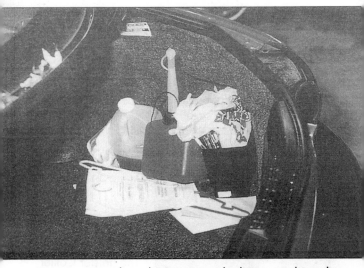

During a search, police recovered other paraphernalia
from Carol Giles's car, including the can of gasoline
used to burn the body.

Carol Giles rode around with Billiter's body in the trunk of her car the day after the murder, before dumping it.

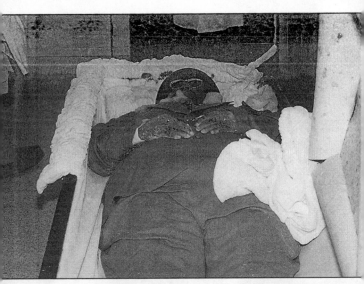

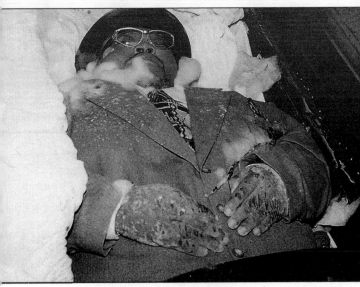

The body of Jessie Giles was exhumed to check for heroin residue that would prove his wife had murdered him. Note the decomposition of the skin on his hands. (*Photo courtesy Oakland County Medical Examiner's Office*)

cars investigating a homicide, no nothing. Tim pulled in the lot across the street. They parked and got out. Tim wanted to see the condition of the body. Carol shoved her hands down deep in her pockets to keep them warm. She zipped her coat so far up, she didn't have any neck exposed to the bitter wind that was whipping off the river.

Tim stuck his arm through her arm, and stuck his hands in his pockets, saying, "C'mon, let's go this way." And like two lovers out for a middle-of-the-night stroll, instead of two murderers returning to the scene of the crime, they crossed the street, entered the park, and jogged down the snow-covered path.

The idea, he explained, was to walk past Nancy's body to see if any of it had burned. He didn't know if anybody was out there looking for them, but if she saw somebody, Carol should pretend she was scared.

Carol didn't have to pretend.

From a few yards away, they walked past Nancy's body, but they were too far away to tell if any of it had been damaged by fire. It looked like it had been. However, being that it was so dark, and it had started to snow again, she couldn't see what part of it had burned, or if it was just the blanket or nothing at all.

What she wanted more than anything was to get the hell out of there. They continued walking, down to the river. The water gurgled in the darkness. Tim said he wanted to hug her.

She let him hug her, but what he was really doing while they embraced was looking around to see if anyone was in the area watching them. After a few minutes of simulated necking, he grabbed her arm and led her along the river, through the dense undergrowth.

Tim followed a serpentine course around the river and back up the street. They found themselves on a road that bent around to some public housing projects. They trotted now, around the back of the projects, cut in front of an empty field, then walked beside a fence.

"Don't walk too fast," Tim warned.

She was taller; he had trouble keeping up. Carol just wanted to get the hell home to her kids.

"Don't look so scared. Don't walk fast. Slow down."

Tim grabbed her arm. He pulled at her to slow down. Soon they were at the car. Relieved to be inside, Tim shot the engine to life, threw the heater on full blast, and tooled over to Uncle Sammy's again. While Tim and his uncle and the girls smoked some, Carol went into the bathroom. When she got out, Uncle Sammy asked her what time it was.

Carol looked at her watch. It was 4:25 A.M. She had been away from her kids, with no one to take care of them, for 4 1/2 hours. She reminded Tim that the kids were home alone.

By the time they left, it was a quarter to five. But Tim still didn't hurry. He drove nonchalantly around town, past favorite haunts, until he got back on the interstate and headed south.

"Do you feel like you're being followed?" Tim asked.

The truth was, she didn't, but she was afraid to disagree with him. Tim seemed so unstable.

"Yeah," she lied.

Tim got off the highway at the last exit before they left the outskirts of Flint behind. He drove around, figuring he'd lead his pursuers on a wild-goose chase until he spotted them; then he'd lose them.

"Any cars follow us off the freeway?" he asked.

Carol turned and looked. No, there was no one behind. Just empty road. Tim kept driving around and then went into an all-night car wash. They pulled into a washing stall.

"Ain't this gonna look suspicious, you going to the car wash at five-thirty in the morning?"

Tim didn't think so. He backed the car up to the vacuum area and stopped. Snaking the pipe inside the car, he began vacuuming. He vacuumed the floor and the mats. He went back and opened the trunk. Nancy's shoe was still there. Tim threw it in the Dumpster. Then he was gone. Carol didn't see him. Where had he gone? Carol looked out the window, trying to see where he was, and then she turned around.

It was like he had materialized in front of the

car. She didn't know how long he had been standing there. But he appeared like he was looking to see if somebody was following them. He saw nothing and got back behind the wheel. They were on their way home.

Carol nodded off on the way. Tim woke her up. He asked her what she was thinking. She opened her eyes to snow blowing in sheets. They were still on the interstate. Tim asked her again what she was thinking.

"Nothing. I'm tired, ya know, I'm just tired."

And then Tim stopped talking to her, questioning her. He was running down. They were just cruising through the night with their problems behind them, left back there in a Flint park, hopefully obscured by flame. Again, Carol drifted off.

Something jerked her awake. Something in her brain was telling her, warning her, not to go to sleep. She sat up and lit a cigarette, smoked for a few minutes and stubbed it out.

Tim got off at the exit for Dixie Highway/Waterford. Despite her best efforts, she fell asleep for a few minutes.

"We're in the driveway," said Tim.

Carol looked up. They were home. She looked at her watch—a quarter to seven! She had to get the kids up for school. But Tim had other ideas first.

"Get Nancy's stuff together. Her bags and all her stuff," said Tim.

He wanted to get rid of any trace that she'd

been there. Carol got Nancy's purse, coat and all her other stuff. When she had finished, there were three bags sitting on the living room floor. Tim came out of their bedroom carrying a duffel.

"I'm going back to Flint. I'll get rid of all this stuff there."

Tim carried it all out to the Caddy and put it in the trunk. He said he'd call her later. Tim pulled out and onto the street, turned the wheel and was soon out of sight.

After he was gone, Carol waited a few minutes and got the kids up. Apparently, they had slept all through the night because they didn't say anything. She dressed them for school and got them on the bus, as usual, at 7:40 A.M. And then she went upstairs and fell into a sound sleep.

Carol awoke at 1:30 P.M. and went to the bathroom. When she finished her business, she looked at the caller ID and didn't see a number that looked like a Flint number. Kind of hungry, she got some crackers, began eating them, and drifted off to sleep again.

"Hello, is anybody home?"

It was L'il Man's voice. The kids, they were home. It must have been after three o'clock.

"Mom, we're home," said L'il Man, who was suddenly standing in her doorway. Jesseca was standing beside him.

"Mom, Aunt Maddie called. She's on the way," said Jesseca.

"Maddie" was Jessie's sister Madeline.

A few minutes later, Maddie came over to take the kids to the mall. She helped the kids on with their clothes. When they were just out the door, she turned and told Carol, "I forgot. My mom was trying to call you. She couldn't get through. Call her."

Carol hesitated for a second before saying she would. Then Maddie and the kids left and for the first time in days, Carol was alone. She fell back to sleep.

The phone woke her up. It was Tim. He told her to get up to Pontiac, to meet him at a store there. He sounded anxious.

"And bring my black shoes."

Carol raced down into the basement where Tim had left his shoes, the ones he'd been wearing when they killed Nancy and dumped the body. She put them in a shoe box and threw them on the front seat of the car and took off. Inside of an hour, they were meeting in a parking lot behind a fast-food restaurant in Pontiac.

Carol got out and sat down in the passenger side of the Caddy. She put the shoes down on the floorboards.

"They found Nancy's body."

Carol was startled.

"How do you know?"

Tim said that when he was over at his uncle's house, something told him to drive by the park.

He drove by and saw the yellow crime scene tape and the Oakland County Sheriff's cars.

Looking at the cops swarming around the crime scene, he realized that the whole time he had been driving around, he had Nancy's stuff in the car. It was all the stuff Carol had gathered up and thrown in the trunk. And Tim had forgotten to get rid of it. He turned around and drove away from the crime scene as casually as he could. He threw the clothing and other belongings in several Dumpsters along the way back.

Carol wanted to know what they would do now. Tim said they had to get rid of the curtains that matched the bedspread in which they had wrapped Nancy's body. They didn't want the cops matching them up.

Carol said she would do so, and Tim said he'd get rid of the shoes. Then he reminded her to get rid of the shoes she was wearing when they killed Nancy.

"I'll call you later, Carol."

They separated. Tim drove back up toward Flint to get rid of his shoes and the other evidence; Carol drove home.

Back at the house, Carol pulled the matching curtains off the windows, including the curtain ties, and threw them in a garbage bag along with the white shoes she had on when they killed Nancy. Then she threw the bag in the trunk of her car. She looked at her watch: 6:15 P.M.

She drove up the street, down the block; she really wasn't sure where she was going, just looking for a good place. Suddenly she felt queasy. She pulled off to the side of the road, opened her door, and threw up. She wiped her mouth, looked up, and realized where she was.

Kmart. She saw it off on the right. Yeah, that was a good place.

She pulled into the lot. It was a cold November night. Few cars were parked. Business was slow.

She put the stuff in a Dumpster behind the store and then drove straight home. By the time she got back, she had missed Tim's call. But it was on the machine.

"Meet me at the Orchard Lake Car Wash," said Tim's voice.

It was a local car wash. A few minutes later, she was there. Tim was already washing the Caddy. He told her that she needed to get rid of the acid on the shelf. She had to go back to the house as soon as she left and get rid of the acid and the syringes, too.

"But the kids."

Putting it mildly, it would be difficult to get rid of the murder weapon with her kids around.

"I told Jesseca I'd call around nine."

She might want to stay with her aunt, which would make things easier. She looked at her watch. It was just nine o'clock. Her cell phone connected her up instantly. Turned out that her daughter wanted to stay the night at Aunt

Maddie's. That was good, but what about L'il Man? And then she had to make sure she could rendezvous with Tim later. It was all so dizzying. Finally she came up with a plan to get rid of the acid while the kids were out with their aunt and then drive back to Flint to be with Tim.

Her luck held. A 9:30 P.M. call prompted L'il Man to say that he would stay at his aunt's, too. Carol drove back, observing all the speed limits. She'd get the acid and the syringes, put them in the car, get rid of them, and then meet Tim in Flint.

As she came abreast of her house, it looked like a car was coming out of her driveway, but she wasn't sure. It turned left and then went down a little ways, and then it turned around and went into the driveway again. Instead of going right into her driveway, she kept going, drove past her house, and soon realized that they had turned into her neighbor's driveway instead.

That was okay, nothing to worry about.

She turned around, came back, and went into her house. She stuck the needles in her coat pocket and grabbed the acid bottle. She came back upstairs and went to her room, where she grabbed the scale that Jessie used to use to weigh the drugs and the remainder of the crack she'd had on hand.

On her way out, she remembered that she had some Henessey cognac and Pepsi in the fridge, so she grabbed that and put the bottles in a brown paper bag. She checked the caller ID and saw that somebody had called from Nancy's mom's house. She called Nancy's mom back.

Phyllis Burke said that they had found Nancy's body. She'd been murdered. Carol feigned shocked disbelief. Carol heard the beep of call waiting on Burke's line.

"You answer the phone and I'll call you tomorrow," she told Mrs. Burke.

She hung up the phone. Time to get the hell out.

Outside, she got into the Caddy. She started it up and was ready to back up when a car pulled in behind her. Carol thought that maybe it was someone who was lost. She was going to back up toward their lights so she could see who it was, but then they flipped on their lights to show her it was actually a police car.

She turned off the engine and stepped out of the car. Detective Kevin Shanlian identified himself.

He began searching her pockets. He found the needles and the scale. He wanted to know what the bottle in her hand was. He took it and looked at the label. It was hydrochloric acid. He wanted to know if she had any drugs. Scared, not thinking, she replied, "Yes," and she handed them over. Another cop had come up behind the first one, also in plainclothes.

"Why don't we go into the house and talk?" said the second cop.

Together, they went into the house.

They tried coaxing her to talk, but Carol wouldn't bite. She had nothing to say except she had just finished talking to Nancy's mother.

Shanlian wanted to know what had happened to Nancy. She said she didn't know. He asked if he searched her house, would he find evidence of a crime, and Carol answered quickly that he wouldn't.

She gave him permission to search. He didn't place her under arrest, just escorted her out to his car to talk while the other officers, a few uniforms included, searched her house. She also cooperated by letting him summon the crime lab to do a sweep of the interior.

Soon after, he took her down to the station for questioning, where she began to write out her first statement.

Ten

It had been four hours in a cramped, hot, stuffy interview room, four hours of a sordid tale that implicated Carol Giles directly in the murder of Nancy Billiter. You didn't have to be Sherlock Holmes to figure out she was no longer a witness but a principal.

Messina asked Carol to stand up. When she did, he told her that she was under arrest for the murder of Nancy Billiter.

"But—"

"Just listen. You have the right to remain silent. If you give up your right to remain silent, anything you say can and will be used against you in a court of law. You have the right to the presence of an attorney. If you cannot afford one, the court will appoint one for you. Do you understand these rights?"

"Yes," said Carol.

Messina put the cuffs on her.

"Okay."

Messina did not want Carol lodged in West Bloomfield, where Collier already was. It was a small jail; it would be too easy for them to talk to each other, to get their stories straight. Instead, he called in another favor and found her accommodations in a cell in the Oakland County Jail. But before she got there, he wanted her to make a few stops first.

Carol had given Messina a lot of information in her statement about where the evidence of the homicide had been secreted in various Dumpsters throughout the county. He sent her out with a few officers to recover that evidence, which they eventually did. Once that was done, she was taken to her cell in the Oakland County Jail.

Prisoners have rights, even when incarcerated. One of those rights is the ability to make phone calls during recreation periods. That night, Carol made a phone call.

At Phyllis Burke's house, the phone rang. Nancy's mother picked it up.

"Will you accept a collect phone call from Carol Giles?" the operator asked.

Burke looked down at her caller ID. The digital readout was OAKLAND COUNTY JAIL.

Burke hung up and called her daughter Susan. She told her that Carol was the one and that she should come over right away. Susan didn't understand, but she came over quickly. When her daughter arrived, Burke said that she thought it was Carol who killed Nancy.

Burke explained that she had just gotten a collect phone call from Nancy. She was in the

Oakland County Jail. What would she be doing there—unless she'd killed Nancy?

Susan paused to think.

"Mom, call the police and tell them what's going on. Make a report."

Saturday night, November 15, 1997. Tim Collier was definitely not partying, though he would have liked to if he were on the outside. Instead, he had a lot of time to think in his cell in the West Bloomfield lockup. He kept wondering where Carol was; no one had brought her in. That meant only one thing.

She was free because she'd ratted him out.

The woman he had killed for, the woman he had loved, the woman he had trusted, had ratted him out. While Michigan didn't have the death penalty, the state legislature had made it law that if you were convicted of first-degree murder—the crime he was charged with—you would get life without parole.

That would be it. Conviction meant no more partying, no more girls, no more anything. Unless he spoke up, he was going down for murder one—and Carol was going to walk.

Tim was nothing if streetwise. He knew better than to talk to a cop without an attorney being present. But he was so angry that Carol had ratted him out that he was willing to waive his right to have an attorney present while he gave his statement to police.

He was standing at the bars to his cell, looking out at the empty cells around him, at the blank, dark concrete walls, up at the fluorescent lighting, when he saw the jailer on duty come in.

Officer Henry Peitz entered the lockup area to assist in moving a female prisoner from cell #5 to cell #4. As he passed cell #1, the occupant, Tim Collier, called out to him.

"Can I ask you a question?"

Peitz nodded.

"Is Carol Giles incarcerated? She is not locked up in here?"

"No, she's not locked up in jail. Should she be?"

"Yes," Tim responded immediately. "I've done good and bad things in my life," Tim began philosophically, "but that was a setup and I wasn't responsible for this crime."

Peitz patiently explained to Collier that Carol had provided a detailed written statement "that only incriminated you."

Collier said that he didn't understand, that the cops had asked him the wrong questions.

"What if something else happened?" Collier said casually. "Can you prove it after someone has been buried, that they've been killed?"

Typing up Carol's second statement took a while. By the time Mike Messina got home, it was midnight. He was just getting into bed when the phone rang. It was Peitz, who told him about the substance of his conversation with Collier.

"Thanks, Henry," Messina replied, and hung up the phone.

Messina couldn't sleep. He kept thinking about Tim's question to Peitz: "Can you prove it after someone has been buried, that they've been killed?"

Who was he talking about? If he told them and he wasn't bullshitting, that meant exhumation and autopsy.

But who?

Messina had had the feeling that Carol had left something out. Something still wasn't adding up right, Messina thought. He got up and went out into the living room and put on the TV.

It was late. All that was on were infomercials. It seemed like every one of them had some Englishman hawking housewares or cleaning solutions or some other junk he didn't need. It made it easy to think.

Carol was claiming that the motive for the crime was that Nancy stole some drugs from them while they were on vacation. They came back and in revenge for faking a burglary and stealing from them, they tortured and murdered her.

It really bothered him. He'd been a detective over twenty years and in a few more he would retire. Then he wouldn't have to think about someone's motives, but now he did. And one thing was clear: you don't kill a woman and torture her for stealing. Even if it were true, her booty wasn't the crown jewels, just a small amount of crack. It just wasn't adding up.

Messina turned off the TV and went into his bedroom. He curled up next to his wife and fell into a restless sleep. Next morning, he got up early and made himself a cup of coffee, extra caffeine.

"Can you prove it after someone has been buried, that they've been killed?"

It is common knowledge that murderers usually know their victims. It could be family or friends. So who was close to Carol or Tim or both of them who's dead and buried and could have been murdered?

Messina turned on the TV to get the news and instead was staring at an infomercial of Richard Simmons exhorting a group of fat women to lose weight. Fat women . . . fat men . . . fat man?

Jessie Giles.

Messina called over to the Oakland County lockup and asked that his prisoner, Carol Giles, be transported to West Bloomfield Police Department as soon as possible.

They had a lot more to talk about.

Carol didn't understand what was happening. Or why.

First they put her in one jail and then she was moved to another.

When she got to headquarters, Helton was already there. He had gotten some sleep and was back. Messina had briefed him. Helton put Carol into an interview room.

"What's this about?" she asked.

Helton told her that Sergeant Messina needed to talk to her again to clear up some things. He left and a few minutes later, Messina walked in. He was freshly shaved, showered and dressed. He looked more like a businessman coming to work to process some orders than a cop trying to solve a double homicide.

"Morning," he said, and Carol nodded in reply.

He carried two cups of coffee and a manila folder. Without saying a word, he placed one of the coffees in front of her.

"Thanks," said Carol warily.

He sat down next to her, crowding her a bit. He took a couple of sips of his coffee. While he did so, he kept tapping the manila folder with his fingers.

"Smoke?"

He offered her a cigarette from a pack in his pocket. She declined. Messina got up and reversed his chair, turning it around so he was now straddling it. He still calmly sipped his coffee.

For a full minute, he didn't say a word. Just looked at her.

"Carol, things are just not adding up," he finally said, putting his coffee cup down. "The motive thing is not working out in my head. Something's just not kosher there."

"What do you mean?"

"Well, I don't believe you and Tim would kill Nancy for stealing a lousy bag full of drugs and faking a burglary."

She met his steady gaze just as Tim had advised her. But instead of backing down, he bore in.

"It's not adding up," Messina repeated.

He opened the manila folder and held up a typed sheet of paper.

"That's a copy of the statement Tim gave to us when he was arrested. Read it," Messina suggested, but he made it sound more like an order.

He put it down on the table and Carol picked it up to read. It was the first she had seen of it. Her face sagged as she read it. Afterward, she looked up, clearly shaken, and for good reason.

Tim said that everything was Carol's idea. Carol was the driving force behind Nancy's murder. If the cops believed him, she was facing hard time.

"I want you to look at Tim's statement again," Messina instructed her. "Look carefully at Tim's sworn statement and circle every part of it that isn't true. Then we'll talk about the inconsistencies between his version and yours."

"Okay," she said, and began to circle all the discrepancies, which, she knew, were many. Messina noticed her hand was shaking. Before she was halfway down, Messina interrupted her.

"Carol?"

She looked up.

"Do you think we can prove it, after someone has been buried, that they've been murdered?"

For a split second, nothing happened. Then, at once, her head slumped down, her shoulders dropped. Tears welled up in her eyes. She buried her face in her hands.

"If we gave you a polygraph right here and now, would you pass it?"

She didn't answer for a moment and then said quietly, "I can't believe I killed Jessie."

Messina didn't show any emotion, but inside, he had a broad smile.

"You have to get it out in the open, Carol, before it consumes you," he said, like a father confessor. "No more hiding anything or keeping anything back. If you don't tell a hundred percent, it's like not telling the truth at all."

Messina sensed that despite her deprivations, she still had a conscience. But for a long time, she said nothing. Had he been wrong?

"I'll give you a statement," she said finally.

They took a break and in the interim moved into a large conference room that was lined with law books. On a rectangular oak conference table, around which the brass regularly met, he set up the tape-recording equipment.

When they were ready, he depressed the machine's button to record.

First thing he did was to advise her, once again, of her rights. The last thing he wanted was a conviction overturned on appeal because she claimed she never got her rights. Even though she had been read them three times previously, four with her arrest, it was standard procedure to read them to her every time she was questioned.

After Carol admitted that she understood her rights, she also admitted that Tim was the driving force behind Jessie's murder.

Tim kept cajoling her, urging her on, insisting she kill her husband and end her misery. Finally, Tim supplied her with heroin. He told her to mix it in with her husband's insulin and inject it.

She had and it had worked. Jessie died. Because of his past medical history, the coroner ruled it natural causes.

"Did you leave anything out, Carol?" Messina asked.

"No, this time I told you everything," she answered.

"What can you do to assure us that you told me everything this time?"

"I don't know what I can do, but I can't get out of one without taking the blame for both of them because they coincided with each other."

"Would you pass a polygraph on the story you told me today?"

"On this story, I would, yeah."

"Any doubt in your mind, Carol?"

"No, no doubt at all."

"Was what you told me tonight [about] Tim's participation in the death of Jessie, was that true?"

"Yes."

"Is there anything else you want to tell me?"

"No."

"Did I promise you anything, Carol?"

"No."

Until that moment of her true confession, Carol and Tim had done something to which every criminal aspires.

They had committed the perfect crime.

They had gotten away with murder.

Eleven

Tim Collier was so anxious to implicate Carol Giles that before Messina could even get to him, Collier told Helton the following:

He said that it was Carol who injected Nancy; it was Carol who had killed her. He also said that it was Carol, not him, who had used gasoline and charcoal lighter fluid to ignite Billiter's body in the park in Flint, where they dumped it. As for having sex with Nancy either alive or dead, he denied ever having sexual contact with Nancy Billiter at any time. As for Jessie Giles, he had a lot to tell about that death, too.

On September 28, 1997, Carol Lynn Giles murdered her husband, Jessie Giles, Tim claimed, by lacing his insulin injection with heroin. Previously, Carol had indicated that a girl she worked with had wanted to kill her husband who was a diabetic, but she did not know how to go about it. That is, without raising any suspicion. This girlfriend wanted it to appear that her husband died of natural causes. Collier then suggested that this could be accomplished by lacing his insulin injection with heroin.

But, Tim said, he had no idea that Carol Giles was really talking about her husband.

On September 28, 1997, Carol contacted him by telephone at his home and said, "I did him. But it's taking a long time."

Tim asked her, "Did what?"

And Carol replied that she had injected Jessie with the heroin/insulin, but he wasn't dead yet. Tim wasn't happy that Carol had done this. He had been having an extramarital affair with her, and some people might become suspicious about Jessie's death because they knew of the Collier-Giles affair. Tim said that he had decided to go to California for two weeks until things "cooled off."

Tim's "new" confession was verbal, not written. Helton briefed Messina on its substance and immediately had him brought out to be interviewed in the same room where he'd spoken to Carol. The chair was still warm.

Messina read Collier his rights via the Miranda card. Tim waived them.

"I'll talk to you," he stated.

"Well, you don't have to talk to me if you don't want to."

Collier insisted that he wanted to talk.

"Well, I don't want to talk about the crime you're in jail for now."

Tim waited.

"You're right," Messina began. "Carol did kill her husband, but I need to clear up some things that are bothering me."

Again, Tim waited.

"How did it go that Carol asked you about killing her husband?"

Tim said that Carol and Jessie weren't getting along anymore, and she asked about getting someone to shoot him. He told Carol:

"You can't shoot somebody in West Bloomfield—people will hear and cops will be all over the place. If I was gonna do it, I'd give him heroin, which would make it look like a heart attack."

But it was just an idea, a hypothetical idea, nothing more.

"Doin' it was all her," he stated emphatically.

"Then why'd you get the heroin for her?" Messina asked.

"I didn't know what that was for when I gave it to her," Tim answered sincerely. "I got it in a two for one deal. I didn't know she was gonna kill Jessie. I thought it was for someone else."

"I know that she went to your house right after she did it."

Tim didn't blink.

"I met her down the street," he corrected the cop. "She brought some money and some drugs. Hell, that's all I was interested in."

As for her story to cops when she found the body: "She could make up any story about getting her hair done or anything. It was her thing, not mine."

Messina then asked Tim if he would write out

a statement about what they had just talked about.

"Okay," he agreed, and wrote out his statement.

The statement he wrote left out much of what they had talked about, and Messina asked him if he wanted to write some more.

"It's all there," Tim said, signing the "confession."

Messina witnessed his signature and then had Tim returned to his cell.

They had Carol and Tim for two murders— Jessie's and Nancy's. The one thing that was most important for the jury to understand was why these people had to die. That was something the prosecution would bring out at trial. But putting a murder case together for prosecution is a lot more difficult than convincing a suspect to give you a statement, or statements.

In many instances, the suspect will recant his confession once his counsel has had a chance to talk to him and tell him what an idiot he was in the first place talking to the police. Or maybe the judge throws it out because the suspect was under the influence of alcohol or some other drug at the time. If that's the case, the individual is not responsible for his statements.

Even if the statement stays in, the prosecution is not out of the woods yet. If the jury believes that the suspect was in any way coerced into giving the statement, they not only can discount it, they should discount it.

With the statement out, what are you left with?

That's why, even after a statement is given, the cops continue working the case. The goal is to put together a chain of evidence with the perpetrator as the strongest link. If the statement stays in, so much the better; if it's thrown out, then they have everything else they've gathered.

The autopsy of Nancy Billiter was consistent forensically with the details supplied by Carol about the method of death and disposal of the body. But both Carol and Tim's statements claimed the other was principally responsible for the injections. That left many possibilities.

The jury could believe Carol and convict Tim, giving her a reduced sentence because they sympathized with her "plight" as a woman psychologically and physically abused by her husband, then psychologically used by her boyfriend for his own nefarious ends. Or, they could look at Carol as a "black widow," an awful woman who killed her husband, lied about it, and was really the mastermind behind Nancy's death.

In that scenario, Carol gets convicted and Tim gets the reduced sentence. In the worst case scenario, the jury believes Tim and sets him free while Carol takes the fall.

Messina saw Carol as someone who, "because of her lousy experiences in life, could shut out everything. Nothing mattered. Tomorrow is tomorrow; today is today. She didn't have to plan on anything long distance. You do what you have to in order to survive."

He may have appealed to her conscience to get her to talk, but the detective sergeant didn't believe Carol had a conscience—at least not in the way most people do. In his opinion, Carol was a master of rationalization. It was like Carol was saying, "Yeah, I killed my husband, but it was something that just had to be done"; that was her attitude. As for Nancy: "Yeah, she was my friend, but what could I do?"

What could she do?

How about not pumping acid into the poor woman's veins?

In all his years in police work, Messina doubted he had seen a more painful way to die. It was torture, plain and simple. In Carol's mind, she wasn't thinking about how much she hurt Nancy. Carol was thinking about the end product.

The end product was Nancy's death, but what was the goal of the torture? Bad guys tortured for one of two reasons. Either they enjoyed inflicting pain before the victim was killed, or they were trying to elicit important information before the victim succumbed.

Nancy could have been shot, nice and neat, with one through the head. If they'd done it someplace secluded, like the park in Flint, there would have been no mess and no one the wiser. It might even have been chalked up to a problem Nancy had with some drug dealer.

No, they didn't have to torture her. Messina was convinced that Carol hadn't told the whole truth. He believed that the reason for the torture was that Tim, and maybe Carol, too, was trying to elicit information from Nancy. But what?

Someplace, in his heart of hearts, Messina wanted to believe that this was a sadistic crime that made sense. To believe otherwise meant Tim Collier was a true monster—and true monsters made even experienced cops shiver.

Monster or not, a criminal's motives are complex. No one ever knows the whole truth. It's a goal to aspire to, but it's just that, a goal. Motive, though, wasn't necessary for a conviction. Just facts that a jury believed.

Problem was, while Carol Giles's second statement seemed reliable in terms of means and opportunity, her first was inconsistent. If Collier had a good defense attorney, he would pounce on those inconsistencies to try and show that his client was the victim of an affair gone wrong.

No, they needed a stronger case to guarantee both convictions.

A child's toy, a piggy bank in the shape of a Coke bottle, had started it all. Carol stated she swung and hit Nancy with it. Where was it? It had not shown up in any of the Dumpster searches; yet it, too, was a murder weapon. Tom Helton kept wondering where it was.

With Carol's help, they had recovered the syringes used to kill Nancy, and they had the acid she was carrying out of the house and the stuff she put in the Dumpsters, including the bleach-laden towel Tim had used to smother Nancy. But what about the piggy bank? Helton went over Carol's statements again.

In one of them, Carol said that the piggy bank had originally been on a shelf, where she and Tim placed it in advance of the murder. She had then taken it off the shelf and confronted Nancy with it. Soon after, she struck her. Helton reasoned that if they had not gotten rid of it, and there was nothing in any of their statements to indicate that, it should still be someplace at the crime scene.

On top of his desk, on a large pile of papers, was a thick manila folder. The words on it read BILLITER HOMICIDE. Helton opened the folder and pulled out a bunch of photographs. He laid them flat on his desktop. He spread them out so he could see better.

They were crime photographs. He shuffled them, until he found the ones he wanted.

Helton looked down at shots of the basement, where Carol and Tim killed Nancy. There were all kinds of shots of the Ping-Pong table, the walls, the floor the mattress and box

springs had lain on before they were moved to
the garage's rafters. There was the bookcase. . . .

The bookcase!

In one of the bookcase's lower shelves, Helton spotted a large object, apparently plastic,
shaped like a soda bottle with the Coke logo.
Helton rifled some papers from underneath his
pile and came up with the statement Carol had
given to Shanlian in which she said that she
struck Nancy with a piggy bank "shaped like a
Coke bottle."

Helton immediately notified Messina and
then called Assistant District Attorney Mc-
Namara to obtain a search warrant. He took
the warrant to the 48th District Court and
swore to it before Magistrate B. Smith. With the
warrant thus authorized, he and Messina drove
down Walnut Lake Road to Carol Giles's house.

Inside, the place was empty. Carol and Tim
were in jail; the kids were with Jessie's sister.
They really would have been surprised if anyone was there.

In the basement, they found the Coke bottle
piggy bank on the shelf, exactly as it had been
in the photo. To preserve the evidence, Helton
pulled on a pair of rubber gloves and picked
it up. The base of the bank was cracked and
broken, probably from the impact with Nancy's
face.

The bottle was placed in a large envelope and
transported back to the police department,
where it was tagged as evidence. Then, follow-

ing procedure, Helton took the piggy bank over to the Michigan State Police Crime Lab at Northville, where it would be tested for latent prints, blood, fiber and other substance analysis. Later that day, Helton received the results.

There had been a positive match for Nancy's blood; Carol's prints were also on the bottle. Helton was batting a thousand.

The kids, Jessie Jr. and Jesseca—what did they know about the murders? Were they witnesses? Had their mother said anything to them? The police needed to know.

Helton picked up the phone and called Maddie Marion, Jessie's sister. The kids were staying with her while Carol was in jail. After the usual introductions, Helton requested an interview with the kids. But Marion was very concerned about the children's well-being. She didn't think it a good idea to be interviewed by the police. Neither, it seems, did Carol.

The night she was placed by Helton in Haven, she made calls to her sister-in-law. She knew Maddie to be a great person, a responsible person. And Carol knew she was in deep trouble.

Carol had done everything she could to keep her kids away from the line of fire, from the actual murder and the cover-up. Admittedly, she had left them home alone when she and Tim disposed of the body on Thursday night, November 13. But wasn't that at least better than taking them along?

What was she supposed to have done? Tell Collier, "Tim, I need a baby-sitter. I can't leave the kids alone while we go to Flint to get rid of the body"?

Wham! The barrel of Tim's automatic would have cracked across her cheek and she'd have a broken face like she'd given Nancy. Then where would she be? Maybe Tim would get nuts; he'd go upstairs and do Jessie Jr. and Jesseca, too.

"No witnesses," Tim always said.

No, Carol had done the right thing. As soon as Nancy was out of there, Carol sent the kids to Jessie's sister. For safekeeping. She made plans that if she faced incarceration, Maddie would take Jessie Jr. and Jesseca in. And she had. Now, Marion was telling Helton over the phone that she didn't want the kids to be interviewed.

Helton thought for a moment.

"Mrs. Marion," he said after a long pause. "I understand how you feel and sympathize. I've got kids of my own. What about this? Why don't you meet me at Pete's in West Bloomfield? It's a family restaurant. We can have a cup of coffee there and talk."

Marion thought that was a good idea and agreed.

At the appointed hour, Helton saw a middle-aged, attractive black woman walk into the restaurant. Maybe it was the attitude or the sport jacket, the type cops wear in real life and in the movies, that identified him. Whatever it was, she introduced herself first; they got a table and some coffee.

"The kids," Marion explained, "they've had a rough time of it. Their father died about six weeks ago."

"I know," said Helton sympathetically.

"I feel the children have not recovered emotionally from their father's death, and to question them about a murder, well, that's probably more than they can handle."

Helton explained that this was a very serious situation. They may have knowledge of the murder and he promised to be tactful and understanding when he questioned them.

Marion certainly understood the police's need for information, but the kids hadn't said anything about what had been happening in their house. Certainly, nothing unusual. And they seemed to be okay.

If the kids had been traumatized, Helton felt sure Marion would have mentioned it, which indicated they probably knew and saw nothing. Carol had done a good job of keeping them out of it. Of course, she had killed their father, too.

"Let me know if they make any mention of what took place in their home," said Helton, rising and taking the check.

Marion said she would.

Back in the squad room fifteen minutes later, Helton sat down in his cubicle. His was the one closest to the door. Maybe when he got a little more seniority, he'd get one in the middle of the room. Or maybe an office? He had to smile; he'd need another promotion for that to happen.

The next thing for him to consider was tying Collier in forensically to Billiter's body. Helton called Judge Edward Avadenka from the 48th District Court for the purpose of swearing to a search warrant for blood, saliva and hair samples from Tim Collier. He faxed the warrant to the judge, and after swearing to the fact and signing it, the judge faxed over a signed copy.

Helton took Collier to a local hospital, where he provided the police with hair, saliva and blood, which would be used for DNA comparison tests with any unknown fluids found on Billiter's body and, in particular, her anus.

He went back and reread the autopsy report. On page 4, halfway down, there was the following statement from the medical examiner:

"There is dried blood within and around the anus with superficial tears present at the 9 o'clock and 12 o'clock positions of the anal ring."

Anal tears didn't happen by accident. They happened when a person was sodomized. Contrary to Giles's statement, what if Collier used an object to sodomize Billiter before she died? Or was it his penis?

They needed the results of Collier's DNA testing to rule the latter out, which would leave only the former as the logical conclusion.

PART THREE

PART THREE

Twelve

November 17, 1997

At 4:40 P.M., Sammy Upchurch sat uncomfortably in one of the interview rooms at the Genessee County Sheriff's Department in Flint.

"At about three-fifteen today, you contacted me in reference to your vehicle being towed, is that correct?" asked Kevin Shanlian.

"Yes, I did," Upchurch replied.

"And I stated to you that I was assisting West Bloomfield Township Police in reference to a homicide case and I stated there was some evidence in your vehicle. Is that correct?"

"Yes."

"And when I made that statement, what did you tell me was in the vehicle that was evidence in this case?"

"Probably, could have been that gas can."

"And why did you think it was the gas can?"

" 'Cause I knew my nephew [Tim Collier] had gave me that gas can and some charcoal lighter fluid."

"Okay, and then I advised you that your vehicle was at the Sheriff's Department pursuant for a search warrant being obtained from the West Bloomfield Township Police Department and you advised that you would give us consent to search. Is that correct?"

"That's right."

Helton had called Shanlian and told him of the substance of Giles's statement. He requested that "Tim Collier's uncle Sammy Upchurch" be contacted. Helton said that he was attempting to locate a five-gallon plastic gasoline container and charcoal lighter fluid that were used in the homicide and to which Giles had obliquely referred in her statement.

Shanlian and his partner, Melki, subsequently drove to Upchurch's home, which they easily found through an on-line database. They passed by the house slowly and saw there was an attached driveway. In the vehicle in the driveway, they observed a five-gallon plastic gasoline container. After failing to contact Upchurch by knocking on his door, Shanlian called Helton.

"What do you want to do?" Shanlian asked.

"Why don't we ask the lawyers," Helton suggested.

Shanlian called the Genessee County prosecuting attorney's office. After conferring with one of the assistants there, he was told to have the vehicle towed, until a search warrant could be secured.

While the car was being towed, someone

came up to Shanlian, who was overseeing the operation.

"Hey, I know the guy that owns that car," the guy said.

Shanlian handed him a printed card.

"My number's on there. Have him call me if he wants it back."

The guy looked at it.

"I'll have him call you," he said, and disappeared into the crowd that had gathered to watch the proceedings.

At 3:20 P.M. the same day, Upchurch called Shanlian.

"Yeah, I own that car," said Upchurch.

Shanlian explained that the vehicle had been towed per the request of Detective Thomas Helton, because it contained evidence relevant to the murder of Nancy Billiter.

"Only the gas is evidence," Upchurch stated.

But he agreed to let the detectives search the vehicle without a warrant. They did. After that, Shanlian called Upchurch back and asked him to come in for an interview. Sammy Upchurch said he would.

"Should I bring the lighter fluid, too?" he asked.

"Yes. Bring it in a paper bag," Shanlian answered, which was how Sammy Upchurch happened to wind up at police headquarters that day for his interview.

Shanlian pushed the tape recorder on the table a little closer to Sammy Upchurch.

"So now that you've come in," Shanlian continued, "you've filled out a consent to search your vehicle? Is that correct?"

"Yes."

"And I advised you you're currently not under arrest at this point, not under any force or coercion, you've given us permission freely?"

"Yes."

"Then the second time I called you back, you asked me if you could bring another item down?"

"Right."

"What was that item?"

"Charcoal starter fluid."

"And why did you think that item was involved in this case?"

"He gave that to me when he gave me the gas. Asked me did I want the charcoal fluid and some gas, but he wanted the gas can back, though."

"Who are we talking about?" Shanlian asked.

"Tim Collier," Sammy Upchurch answered.

"What relationship is he to you?"

"A stepnephew."

Upchurch went on to describe his stepnephew's first visit on the afternoon of the murder. While Carol waited for him back in West Bloomfield, Tim went to his uncle's.

"He was by hisself and he wanted to take a bath."

"Was he bloody or anything?" Shanlian asked.

Upchurch said he wasn't. Collier stayed maybe two hours, took his bath, decided to leave, and said he may come back later.

"Did he leave any clothes at your house?"

"No, he hadn't. He took his clothes with him. On his back."

Shanlian remembered that Collier's crime scene clothes had been recovered during the search that Giles had led the cops on before she was taken to the Oakland County lockup.

"Did he have a change of clothes with him?"

He had, Upchurch answered. In a duffel bag.

"When was the next time you saw Mr. Collier?"

"Maybe around nine or ten that same evening."

Shanlian knew he had to be off. Carol said it was past midnight when they got there. He couldn't alter the man's statement, but unless he clarified it, a good defense attorney could rip holes in it because of inconsistencies with Carol's statements.

"Okay, it was late at night, it was dark out?" Shanlian asked.

Upchurch said it was.

"And he comes by with his girlfriend?"

Upchurch said yes. He'd seen her with him before. The girlfriend was white, a blonde, slim. She was tall and wore glasses. Clearly, it was Carol Giles.

"We were just setting and in the living room, just talking anyhow, they were just talking about, you know, everyday things really. Really, nothing really that I can remember."

"Did they seem agitated or upset?"

Upchurch said no.

"Did they appear nervous?"

He said they didn't appear nervous, either.

"Did they seem like they were sad over something?"

"No, they just seemed like they were just regular, you know, just like nothing happened."

"Were they smoking crack cocaine at that point?"

"Yes, well, he was; I never seen her smoke anything. Anyway, he went back in the bathroom a couple of times. I heard the lighter flick while he was in the tub."

Apparently, Collier had decided to take another bath. Maybe he was washing Billiter's blood off.

"So he was smoking crack there and they were just acting normal? How long did you talk to them?"

"Maybe fifteen or twenty minutes or so."

"Then what did you do?"

"I went to my bedroom and watched TV. I was tired. I was sitting on the bed there and that's when he was talking about getting the gas and stuff out of the car. And he comes in and says, 'You want some gas?' He asked me, 'Did I need some charcoal; could I use some charcoal lighter fluid?' I told him, 'Yeah, I could use it.' He said, 'Well, I got some gas,' but he wanted the gas can back."

There was only about a gallon of gas in the gas can, Upchurch remembered. Shanlian knew that the rest of it was back in the park, on Nancy Billiter's body and the trail leading up to it.

It was a good thing that neither Collier nor Giles was a firefighter or arsonist. Otherwise, they would have been successful at burning Billiter and then the cops' job would have been doubly hard.

A burned body was exceptionally hard to identify. If the features were beyond recognition, or the fingers burned to the point they couldn't lift a print, the police had to rely on a forensic dentist to do the ID off the victim's teeth.

Shanlian wanted to know who brought the gas can and stuff in. Upchurch said "the girlfriend" did. Then Sammy Upchurch put all the stuff in the hallway upstairs.

"And that's where [the items] stayed the whole time until I called?" Shanlian asked.

"The lighter fluid did, but the gas can was up there about three hours and I didn't want to take a chance. I was cooking, you know, baking some cakes and pies, but I thought about them."

Uncle Sammy Upchurch hardly seemed like the Martha Stewart type, but who knows? Maybe he was a good chef.

"I had the oven door open," Upchurch continued, "and I didn't want that gas can by my door, so I moved the can myself down to the bottom of the steps. I poured the gallon of gas in my car and put the gas can in my car so the can wouldn't be in my house and put no fumes in my house."

After they gave him the gas, they stayed maybe another hour and then left.

"When was the next time that you saw Mr. Collier?"

Upchurch had gone out on Friday, November 14, but his cousin had stayed over and it was his cousin who said Tim came to visit later that day. They went to a local motorcycle club, hung out there for a while. But all Tim did was visit. He brought nothing with him, left with nothing, and according to the cousin, he discussed nothing unusual or suspicious.

"Has Tim contacted you since?"

"No."

"Are you involved in any way, including helping dispose of the body of Nancy Billiter?"

"No!"

"Did you assist Mr. Collier or Mrs. Giles in any way with this homicide?"

"No!"

"Did you have any knowledge of this homicide prior to newspaper reports or TV reports?"

"No, I didn't."

"At no time did Mr. Collier advise you that he had committed a homicide?"

"No, he didn't."

"At no time did Mr. Collier appear upset or nervous or sad or anything like that in that time frame that you dealt with him?"

"No. But I did hear one thing, though."

Shanlian was curious.

"Which was?"

"My cousin told me that before they went to the motorcycle club on Friday, Tim was over there and Tim doesn't usually drink, but that night he did."

"So he drank quite a bit that night?"

"That's all."

At approximately 5:10 P.M., Shanlian released the vehicle back to Sammy Upchurch so he could drive home. The search of Upchurch's vehicle had produced no further evidence.

After Upchurch left, Shanlian sat down at his cluttered desk to think.

Collier had given the can containing the gasoline he'd poured over Nancy Billiter's body to his uncle Sammy, who had, in turn, secreted it in his car. And that night, when Collier went up to Flint while Giles slept, before he came back to dispose of the body with her, he got drunk with another relative. Yet, Tim Collier didn't drink.

Why did Tim Collier drink the night after they got rid of Nancy Billiter? Did he have a conscience, too? Did he drink out of guilt for causing Nancy's death? Or was he drinking in celebration of it? Was he even capable of celebration?

The one thing Shanlian had no doubt of was that Tim Collier was capable of double homicide.

November 17, 1997

The Oakland County Prosecutor's Office issued warrants for both Carol Giles and Timothy Collier. The charges were first-degree murder and conspiracy to commit murder.

They were arraigned in Judge Edward Avadenka's 48th District Court. Sitting in on the proceedings were Phyllis Burke, Nancy's mother; and Stephanie Johnson, Jessie's daughter, whom the kids referred to as Aunt "Stephi." As they were led into court in their orange prison jumpsuits, Carol Giles and Tim Collier did not talk to each other.

"How do you plead, Mr. Collier?" Judge Avadenka asked.

"Not guilty to both charges," Tim announced.

"Mrs. Giles?"

"Not guilty, Your Honor."

"Your Honor, considering the seriousness of the crime, I ask that the suspects be held without bail," said assistant Oakland County prosecutor Kate McNamara.

"Suspects held without bail, pending a preliminary examination [formal arraignment] on December first."

He banged down his gavel. Outside the courtroom, reporters jockeyed to get statements from the principals.

"How long they took [to murder Nancy] is unclear, but she did suffer," said McNamara. "They accomplished their objective, which was murder, and they took their time doing it."

"Everyone assumed [Jessie] died of natural causes," added deputy Oakland County prosecutor James Halushka. "Now we're going to have to petition a court to have his body exhumed."

The medical examiner had told prosecutors, Halushka said, that he could employ various toxicology tests to determine if Giles died from a heroin overdose.

Stephanie Johnson, twenty-three, who had come to court after prosecutors told her that her stepmother was a suspect in her father's death, told reporters that Carol received a significant inheritance when Jessie died. That implied a financial motive for the killing.

"She got a boyfriend pretty quickly. But there were kids involved. Whoever this man is, he's good," Johnson observed, implying Collier had conned his way into the Giles family. She blamed Tim Collier for masterminding the killing.

Reporters moved down the courtroom corridor to speak to Phyllis Burke. She recalled a conversation she had had with her daughter soon after Jessie died.

"Nancy told me, 'Mom, Carol's the best friend I've got and I'm not going to let anything happen to her.' This just makes me so sick."

Eddie Grant, Nancy's boss at the restaurant, said that he gave Nancy a warning before she died.

"I told her, 'I know she's [Carol's] got problems, but you should try to get as far away as possible from her.' She had a big heart and that kind of turned out to be her downfall."

Late that day, Helton passed by South Boulevard Station on his way home from work. In the twilight, a sign on the window out front said, WE MISS YOU, NANCY.

November 19, 1997

Dr. Dragovic, the county medical examiner, was advised of the suspicious circumstances of Jessie Giles's death. He checked his records and confirmed that an autopsy had not been done and issued a letter requesting that Jessie's remains be exhumed.

Messina met with Maddie Marion and told her what was going on. If the family didn't want an autopsy, the police would have to get one anyway, but it was a lot easier, and less painful, if the family went along.

They did. In his report, Messina wrote that Maddie gave permission to exhume "the body of Jessie Giles for investigative purposes." This information was then faxed to the prosecutor's office, where an official exhumation order was prepared.

November 22, 1997

Maddie Marion looked around the home. It was empty now, dusted for fingerprints, stripped of evidence, sterilized by the presence of cops and lawyers and medical examiners and all the rest. But to her, it had once been a home, her brother's home—her brother and sister-in-law's and her niece and nephew's.

The children. What would become of the children?

It was a question that Maddie and her husband, Philip, had answered by opening their home to them. Susan Garrison, Nancy's sister, later claimed that after the kids came to live with Maddie and Philip, Carol called the couple from jail.

According to Garrison, during that conversation, Carol told her kids that she had killed Nancy and she was going to jail for a real long time. Maddie and Philip would take care of them as long as she was gone.

"Mrs. Marion?" said Tom Helton. "You wanted to remove some personal property?"

That's why Maddie was there.

"Just let us know when you leave," Helton advised, and then he was out the door, leaving her alone to her memories and her grief.

November 25, 1997

The temperature was in the low twenties with a wicked wind blowing that forced the windchill well below zero. The sky was gray and overcast; snow was in the forecast. The ground was as hard as a rock.

Officer Tom Helton shivered inside his overcoat. He looked down at a newly dug gravesite dusted with snow. The grave was only seven weeks old, but its occupant could not rest in peace. Not until the police knew for certain how he had died.

"We're ready," said a workman to Helton.

In Helton's inside jacket pocket was the court order.

"Your Honor," Helton told the district court in Pontiac a day before, "we have reason to believe that the decedent was murdered."

The judge had granted the police department an exhumation order to proceed to Perry Mount Park Cemetery for the purpose of digging up Jessie Giles.

"Go ahead," said Helton, and the workman signaled.

The backhoe moved in. It paused momentarily on the raised plot of ground that was supposed to be Jessie Giles's final resting place. Then it descended with a roar and dug into the ground, moving it aside like it weighed nothing.

It only took a few minutes; then Helton was able to look down into the hole and see the metal casket that contained Jessie's body. The backhoe backed off and workmen from Classic Removal, the company doing the exhumation, jumped into the hole, where they attached lines to a crane. When the lines were secured, the crane fired up and slowly lifted the casket containing the huge body, minus whatever weight he may have lost in the prior weeks.

The casket was put on a rolling gurney that county workers wheeled over to a van, where they slid it inside. The doors were slammed shut; one of the workers tapped the door a couple of times and the van pulled out. Helton got into his car and drove out of the cemetery, thinking what a gloomy place this was on a late-fall day.

It only took him a few minutes to get to the Oakland County Municipal Complex, where he headed straight for the morgue. Dr. Victor Ehrlich was in charge of the postmortem. The casket lay on the same gurney that had taken it from the grave to the van. Helton watched as Ehrlich opened it.

Jessie Giles was dressed like he was going to a party. He wore a bright green suit with a breast pocket handkerchief, matching shirt and tie, and gold-framed glasses. Jessie's stylin', Helton thought. Carol sure sent him off in style.

The casket had been airtight and it looked like decomposition had been minimal. Ehrlich had his assistants strip the body and carefully catalogue each piece of clothing.

"On my count," said Ehrlich, "one, two, three." And with everyone huffing and puffing, they lifted Jessie and placed him on the autopsy table.

The doctor opened Jessie up. Removing the heart from the chest cavity, the coroner examined it carefully. While noting what poor shape it was in, he could find no recent scarring. Jessie Giles had not died of a heart attack. Carol's contention that he died of a heart attack was now proven to be false.

Ehrlich took tissue samples from Jessie's liver, heart and brain. Each of those organs would retain vestiges of morphine, a heroin derivative, if heroin had been used to overdose him. The samples were labeled, put into evidence containers, and sent out for toxicology examination. The body was sutured closed.

Morgue attendants then dressed Jessie in his burial clothing, placed his body back in the coffin, and sealed it airtight. The workers from Classic Removal drove it back to the cemetery, where the body was quickly taken from the van and placed back in the ground. The backhoe moved in and efficiently filled the grave with the burial dirt. That night, it snowed. The next day, anyone passing by saw nothing unusual save for a mound of freshly dug earth covered with snow.

A few days later, the toxicology results came back. Jessie's tissues showed a high concentration of morphine.

"Anytime you inject heroin into the body, it changes to morphine," Dragovic, the Oakland County medical examiner, explained to the *Detroit News.* Jessie was "injected [with] a substantial amount and caused rapid intoxication" and then death, Dragovic continued.

Since Jessie wasn't an addict, the only logical conclusion was exactly what Carol Giles had said in her statement: she had given him a heroin overdose when Jessie thought he was just getting his usual insulin injection.

That still meant that Tim Collier was not directly tied into Jessie's death. It was Carol's word against his. She said he supplied her with the heroin and expertise to commit the crime; he said she was lying.

It would be up to a jury to decide.

Another bulldozer picking up frozen earth. Another gray day. Another graveside.

As Nancy's sister Susan Garrison looked around, she saw a lot of people. Nancy Billiter had gotten to know a lot of patrons at the places she worked. They knew her to be what she was—a very caring person, the kind who would do anything for you if she could.

That was it, Susan thought. She was always for the underdog. Always root for the underdog.

Just before she died, Nancy was going to college to be a nursing assistant. She'd always wanted to be a nurse. She'd been to school before but never completed the coursework because something, more or less, got in the way. This time—the last time—it had been death.

The coffin was lowered out of sight into the deep, dark grave.

Bill Bernhard had heard about Nancy Billiter's death. He had seen a report on the news and had gone to her funeral. And, he felt, he knew something of value. Bernhard called up Helton and they met at South Boulevard Station.

The bar was the same as Nancy had left it. Only there was an emptiness now, a listlessness among the patrons and staff, that only time could cure.

"I was here on November twelfth," Bernhard told Helton.

"What time?" Helton asked.

"In the evening, during Nancy's shift."

"Know her long?"

"We were old friends. I knew her, twenty years. Nancy told me that her roommate had returned from California. She didn't have her friend's car any longer, 'cause her friend wanted to use it now. She needed to find a ride home."

"What happened?"

"Well, I don't have a car, either. But the bartender Dawn—well, she let me take her car and drive Nancy home with it."

"Stop anyplace along the way?"

"No. We got back to the home in West Bloomfield, where she was staying with her friend, at about eleven o'clock."

That jibed with everything Carol Giles had told them and would help establish Carol's credibility in court.

"I walked in the house with her. Nancy had told me about the break-in there and I wanted to make sure she got in safely."

Why would Nancy lie about the break-in to anyone but Tim and Carol if it didn't really happen?

"I was inside with her about four minutes," Bernhard continued. "Nancy hung up her coat and she told me that her friend and boyfriend were there in the bathroom. The door was closed but the light was on."

Helton reasoned that they might have gone inside when they heard Bernhard talking to Nancy. They could have heard them when they came up the driveway. The last thing the murderers would have wanted was someone else showing up and spoiling their plan. Tim Collier would have known that if they killed Nancy and her body was later discovered, Bernhard would be a witness who could put him at the scene of the crime.

"I left to take Dawn's car back to her at the bar. After a short while there, I caught a ride with a friend and went home. I called the bar the next day in the late afternoon to see if Nancy was working," Bernhard continued. "Around three or four I called. Anyway, I was told that she had not shown up for work that day. I called her at home two or three times during the course of the evening and never got an answer."

Of course he didn't. Nancy was dead in the trunk of Carol Giles's car.

Thirteen

The beleaguered Detroit Lions played their home games in the Pontiac Silverdome. Why that indoor stadium had been located in Pontiac, though, was anybody's guess.

Pontiac was a middle-class town, hardly the sort of place to support the big-buck tickets and luxury boxes that are the financial mainstays of National Football League teams. West Bloomfield Township, with its more affluent citizens, would have been a much better place to put the stadium. Rich people, however, are usually smart enough to figure out that they would rather have a disruptive influence like a football stadium in another, albeit less affluent, community. They can just drive there in their BMWs and then leave after the game.

It is doubtful that the workers in the county office complex, of which the prosecutor's office is a part, had season tickets to the Lions. The games were much too expensive for them to afford.

Within the county office complex is a white building. At the top of a hill in the middle of the city of Pontiac, it looms like a modern monolith. This is the Oakland County Prosecutor's Office. Inside the building in his small corner office, Chief Prosecutor John Skrzynski looked down on the area below. It was a large county.

Whoever was murdered in that vast urban sprawl, sweeping out toward the horizon, their file came across his desk.

Skrzynski picked up the folder marked JESSIE GILES and NANCY RAE BILLITER. He opened it and began to read.

The first killing disposed of a problem for the killers. The second—well, it still remained a mystery. Skrzynski didn't buy the motive Carol had laid out—Nancy was killed because of the faked burglary—any more than Messina did. The prosecutor was particularly incensed at the savage way Billiter had been killed. That was something that could work to his advantage at trial.

Juries like to identify with the decedent. If the prosecution could downplay Nancy's drug problems, she could be a very sympathetic victim, fitting the classic "wrong place at the wrong time" scenario that could happen to anybody. The fact of her torture made it more likely that the jury would go for personal identification, which, hopefully, would lead to two convictions.

But before a trial could take place, the suspects needed to be officially arraigned. Since the paperwork was still being put together on the Jessie Giles murder, the decision was made to arraign the defendants for Nancy Billiter's murder first.

January 6, 1998

The formal arraignment for Nancy Rae Billiter's death was supposed to happen in December 1997, but because it was taking so much time to put the toxicology and other forensic evidence together, and to give the defense equal time to examine that material, the arraignment had been moved to January.

The crowd in Michigan's 48th District Court waited anxiously for the defendants to be brought in. It was the type of tension that makes your stomach turn over, the knowledge that something was going to happen, something bad, and there was no way to stop it. It was the knowledge that even though the crimes were over, they were about to be relived, in the courtroom, in all their bloody detail.

In the courtroom crowd was Nancy's brother, Doug. Like all siblings, they had had their disagreements. They had had one before Nancy's death, a big fight, sister Susan Garrison remembered.

"She died before they could make up," said Susan. "This time there was no making up."

Suddenly the door at the side of the courtroom opened. Clad in orange prison jumpsuits and manacled at wrist and ankle, Tim Collier and Carol Giles shuffled in and were escorted by the guards to their lawyers at the defense table. On the other side was the prosecutor, John Skrzynski.

An arraignment is anything but a formality. It is the time the state's feet are held to the fire, where they must prove to the court's satisfaction that they have enough evidence to go to trial, where they hope to get a conviction.

Likewise, it is the suspects' opportunity to question the validity of the state's evidence. If the suspects can prove the state does not have enough to hold them, or if the state illegally obtained or manufactured evidence, they walk.

In a sense, the arraignment is a mini trial, where each side has an opportunity to call the witnesses they plan to present at the actual event. What makes it interesting is that, like the end of a poker game, each side is forced to show what they have in their hand.

As far as Skrzynski was concerned, he was holding a straight flush.

"The state calls Sergeant Mike Messina."

Messina came forward.

"Raise your right hand," said the clerk.

Messina raised his hand.

"Do you swear to tell the truth, the whole truth, and nothing but the truth?"

"I do."

Messina took his seat in the witness box.

Without wasting time, Skrzynski asked Messina to relate the substance of his interview with Carol Giles.

"Tim told Carol to 'stick her,' " Messina testified.

He told the court how Carol Giles and Tim Collier injected Nancy with battery acid and how Collier beat her with his gun. They finally killed her by smothering her with the wet towel.

According to Giles's confession, after Nancy was dead, Collier wondered "what it would be like to have sex with a dead body." Giles told Collier he was "sick," Messina testified. "Tim asked if they could have sex and she said yes."

No mention was made of the tearing in Nancy's rectum indicative of sodomy and the strong possibility that Tim Collier had violated Nancy Billiter just before her death and perhaps stayed inside her afterward. It was just too horrible to contemplate. Besides, they still hadn't gotten back the results of the DNA testing.

They had, however, gotten back the results of the tire analysis at the crime scene. After eliminating the police cars and other support and investigative personnel, there could be no positive identification of any other car at the scene. That meant that, forensically, there was nothing to tie Carol Giles's car to the scene. Messina did not mention that, either, nor was he obligated to.

After Messina came the Oakland County medical examiner, L.J. Dragovic. He testified that it was he who had performed the autopsy that showed eleven puncture burns on Nancy's body. He, too, omitted mention of the anal bruising. It would add nothing to the state's case except make it more gruesome and more difficult for the family.

Some of Nancy's relatives couldn't take what the newspapers the next day described as a "gruesome tale." They walked out of the courtroom; some in tears, never hearing, at least not yet, how Giles and Collier took almost twenty-four hours to dispose of the body, and when they did, how they tried to burn it to cover up the evidence.

"I just can't believe someone could do that to someone else, especially someone who was supposed to be a friend of my sister's," Doug Billiter said afterward.

At the end of the hearing, the court handed down first-degree murder indictments against Timothy Orlando Collier and Carol Giles in the death of Nancy Rae Billiter. The state then made the decision to try the defendants with separate juries, simultaneously, in the same courtroom. While unorthodox, trying two defendants with two juries had been shown to be efficient in other criminal cases in Michigan. The judge agreed.

It meant a little bit of people jockeying when one jury was allowed to hear evidence while the other, for various legal reasons, could not.

But it was efficient, since many of the same witnesses needed to testify in both cases, like the medical examiner, police officers and people who knew the decedents.

As to any lingering doubt that the trials might not take place because one or the other of the defendants would take a plea to lesser charges, Skrzynski quickly erased that possibility.

Giles and Collier were charged with capital crimes. The state might not have the death penalty, but they still took murder seriously. It was capital murder—the worst kind of crime—cold-blooded and premeditated. There was no talk of making a deal to spare the state the expense of two trials.

Besides, Giles had already flipped on Collier, and the self-confessed California gang banger was set for the fall. Skrzynski was betting on Carol Giles's statement holding up at trial.

Unfortunately, sure things do not exist.

Despite what Carol Giles had stated to the cops, when the judge asked her how she pleaded, she had answered, "Not guilty." That meant that her attorney, in any way he could, would try to suppress or downplay her confessions. Plus, Tim Collier had given the police two statements in which he said that she was the murderer, not him.

Who would the jury believe? They wouldn't know until they went to trial.

* * *

January 8, 1998

Helton received a report from the Michigan
State Police Crime Laboratory regarding the
examination of evidence submitted for latent
fingerprints. Examined were the gas can, the
charcoal lighter can, Billiter's driver's license,
which had been found in a search of the Giles
home, and the .32-caliber Titan handgun
found under the seat in Carol's car.

No matches were made with the submitted
comparison prints of Collier and Giles. That
meant that, forensically, none of that evidence
could be tied into either defendant.

Despite this setback, the prosecution pressed
on.

January 9, 1998

Giles and Collier were back in Judge Avadenka's court, to hear a new set of murder
charges, this time for killing Jessie.

Messina testified to Giles's confession, that
she and Collier had conspired to and had killed
Jessie by lacing his insulin with heroin. Dragovic took the stand and said under oath that
tests on tissue samples from Jessie's body
showed a lethal level of morphine.

"Anytime you inject heroin into the body, it
changes to morphine," he explained once
again. "It was injected in a substantial amount

and caused rapid intoxication," then death, he said. Because of Jessie's poor health history, there was no reason to suspect foul play and an autopsy was not done at the time.

Speculating on other causes of death, Dragovic said, "Every other consideration is out of the question in this case. It was a homicide. That's the bottom line."

Tim Collier was not going to go gentle into that good night. Whether he believed it or not, he testified that he wasn't in any way, shape or form involved in the killing of Jessie Giles. He'd had nothing to do with it.

At the end of the hearing, both he and Carol Giles were formally charged with first-degree murder in Jessie's death.

March 2, 1998

The guilt swirled in Carol Giles's mind like a carousel she couldn't get off. There was nothing to look forward to now, except a long prison stretch if convicted. She wouldn't be able to see her kids grow up, go to school, have babies. She'd be stuck in prison someplace, getting old.

Somehow she got a hold of a bottle of Tylenol and ate the pills like candy, hoping she'd take enough to die. But she didn't really want to check out, at least not yet, because she told a prison counselor what she had done.

She was rushed to the POH Medical Center in Pontiac. Emergency room doctors pumped her stomach. Afterward, she was placed on a twenty-four-hour suicide watch.

All of the evidence had been gathered and catalogued in both murders. The state made the decision to press forward with the case against Carol Giles and Tim Collier for murdering Jessie first, and a trial date of June 15 was set, with the trial for killing Nancy set for July. Evidentiary hearings, including pretrial motions, would be heard in May.

Neither Carol Giles nor Tim Collier had any money with which to hire a private attorney. Both defendants were therefore given court-appointed attorneys to work their defense. Representing Carol Giles was John Basch; Howard S. Arnkoff performed the same function for Tim Collier.

The lawyers knew that the whole case came down to Giles's confession. Basch and Arnkoff knew that if they could cast doubt on her statements, one or both clients could walk. Skrzynski knew that with the confession he had a strong case against Carol Giles, but it was not nearly as strong against Tim Collier.

It would always be her word against his, because the case, ultimately, was circumstantial. No blood—so far—or fibers had been found on Collier to tie him directly to either murder. And he continued to deny any wrongdoing.

May 21, 1998

Tim Collier was tired. He was tired and drugged and didn't know what he was saying when he spoke to police after Nancy Billiter's death.

"My head was kind of cloudy," Collier said, stating that he had gone 144 hours straight without sleep. Anything he said to police had been influenced by that lack of sleep and too many drugs in his system.

Collier told all this to Judge Rudy Nichols at the pretrial hearing to determine the admissibility of the statements he made to police after his arrest. It was what prosecutors feared, the "I didn't know what I was saying because I was under the influence" defense.

Nichols listened patiently. But he heard nothing to make him believe that Tim Collier was telling the truth. To Skrzynski's relief, he ruled that Collier's statements were still admissible.

May 26, 1998

It was now Carol Giles's turn to try the same tactic.

Her attorney, John Basch, read the transcript

of the polygraph examiner's interview with Giles and thought he saw some daylight. The record showed that when Chester Romatowski, the polygraph operator, questioned Carol prior to the test, their conversation went like this:

"Are you withholding any information?" Romatowski asked. "Do you want to speak to an attorney?"

"I want to speak to an attorney," Carol answered.

That was it. The interview should have ceased, Basch argued. His client had asserted her right to counsel prior to giving her most incriminating statements. Therefore, questioning should have ceased. Everything she said after that violated her Miranda rights, and the confession should have been thrown out.

When it was Skrzynski's turn, he argued that after Carol Giles said, "I want to speak to an attorney," the record showed that Romatowski answered as follows:

"You may speak to an attorney if you wish or you can speak to a detective."

Carol had thought about her answer and then replied: "I want to talk to the detective."

By agreeing to talk to a detective instead of an attorney, she waived her Miranda rights. The police were therefore under no obligation at that point to provide her with an attorney. He cited case law to prove his point.

After carefully considering both sides, Judge Nichols ruled that Carol Giles had waived her right to an attorney when she gave her statement. She had not been coerced. The confessions stood.

"She confessed; there's a video of the confession, and the jury will hear it," John A. Basch, Carol's attorney, told the press afterward. It was time to put a little spin on things. "But that's only part of the story."

No kidding, thought Skrzynski, listening.

"She intends to testify and fill in the blanks."

Now that was something Skrzynski could look forward to. It was rare for a defendant to testify on her own behalf in a capital case because then the prosecution gets their shot at breaking down their defense during cross-examination. Courtroom confessions only happen on TV, never in real life. Still, a skilled prosecutor can show the discrepancies in the defendant's story while he or she is on the stand.

"I think the jury will be captivated, and the outcome of this case, despite what the prosecutor may believe, is not a foregone conclusion," Basch continued.

John Skrzynski, of course, disagreed.

"The case is pretty strong against Giles because she gave a pretty detailed statement about what happened," Skrzynski told the press when it was his turn. "Collier did also and it's fairly incriminating.

"Since there were no witnesses to Giles's murder except Carol Giles, the case hinges on their testimony. Whatever the jury thinks of their statements is what their decision will be," Skrzynski continued.

Tim Collier, of course, disagreed. He came up with a novel defense. Howard S. Arnkoff, Collier's attorney, told the press why his client should be acquitted.

"He was in Pontiac when Giles was injected," said Arnkoff. "They claim he gave Carol Giles advice, but that isn't true. She allegedly injected her husband first and then called Collier up wanting to know why he wasn't dying fast enough."

Mike Messina sat at his desk and looked back.

It had been nine months since Jessie was murdered. His killers had almost gotten away with it; they still might.

Jessie's wife was in jail for killing him. So was his friend Tim Collier. His children were now living with his sister. It was a lousy situation any way you looked at it.

In the end, Messina knew that there was only one thing left. It was an abstract concept at best, one best left for philosophers and not cops. But once in a while, Messina knew, it happened. It really came out.

The truth.

Fourteen

DNA testing is complicated. It can take months before the results come back. In the Billiter case, when they did, it was not to the satisfaction of the prosecution.

Nancy Billiter's torn anus came back negative for Tim Collier's DNA. None of his fluids were present, not blood, mucus, saliva. That meant that if he had inserted his penis into the body cavity, he had to have been wearing a condom. The other possibility was that she was raped with an unidentified object. Helton had thought it might be the Coke bottle/piggy bank, but that came back negative for Nancy's fluids.

But someone had sodomized Nancy Billiter. She hadn't been anally bruised by accident. That much was clear. Then who had done it, and how had it been done?

Women don't usually engage in forcible sodomy; men do. And Carol had no reason to force herself on Nancy that way. Forcible sodomy shows an inexpressible amount of rage and anger, like the type Tim Collier carried around with him all the time.

If Carol Giles was telling the truth, that she never saw Tim rape Nancy, then there was only one explanation: Collier sodomized Billiter, either with an object or with his protected penis, when Carol wasn't around. When had it happened?

In going back over Carol Giles's first statement, Helton noticed the following interchange between her and Shanlian:

"What happened after Tim and Nancy smoked crack? What time was that?" Shanlian had asked.

"About eleven-thirty. Then about one-thirty, I went upstairs to check on my children, who were sleeping. When I got back to the basement, Nancy was on the bed tied up with nylons and she was screaming," Carol answered.

"What happened then?"

"Nancy's pants leg was off. . . ."

What if, Helton theorized, while Giles was upstairs, Collier sodomized Billiter? He could have used a condom, which he flushed down the toilet afterward. Or maybe he had used an object in the room that hadn't been tested. The basement itself was a combination sleeping area/laundry room/work area, with tools, laundry bottles and other things scattered about; none of these things had been tested for fluids because there were just too many.

There was still another possibility that Helton and the other detectives, even the medical examiner, had not considered because it was just too gruesome to contemplate.

In her statement, Carol Giles clearly stated that when she and Tim Collier left the basement, she thought Nancy Billiter was dead. What if Billiter wasn't?

According to Carol, she and Tim had sex after killing Nancy. Afterward, Carol got the kids up and ready for school. Not knowing that their "aunt" Nancy was lying in the basement dead, they got washed and dressed. Jesseca, though, was sick.

"You have to go to school, honey. You can't stay home," her mother had insisted.

The last thing she needed was her daughter around when they disposed of the body. Carol gave her some Tylenol and reassured Jesseca that she would "feel better."

What if, while Carol was playing "concerned mother," and without her knowledge, Collier slipped down to the basement. The urge to do it with a dead body was just too overwhelming. When he got to Billiter, he turned her over.

Nancy Billiter wasn't dead. She was warm. She was unconscious but alive.

Collier pulled down Billiter's pants and inserted an object into her anus. And he pushed and he pushed and he pushed, tearing the anus and causing the bleeding that would later be noted by the medical examiner.

There is no telling how long Collier might have stayed there. There is no telling when exactly Billiter died. He might have continued to sodomize her even after death; for while the rectal muscles would have relaxed, the physical damage would already have been done. There would be no way to tell, save his confession, that he had continued to sodomize a corpse.

Upstairs, Carol had convinced her daughter to go to school and then walked both kids to the bus stop. When she came back in the house, Tim was sitting there in the living room.

There was a body to deal with in her basement. That's all Nancy was to her now—a body.

Monday, June 15, 1998

It took two days for the voir dire, the part of a trial where juries are questioned about their beliefs, predispositions, knowledge of the case, anything that might impact on their ability to serve on a jury. The defense had the opportunity to challenge jurors and so did the prosecution. And at the end of that time, thirty-two people became jurors—twelve jurors and four alternates for each jury.

Carol Giles watched them walk in and be seated at the side of the courtroom. It was hard on that bright June day, just a few days before the summer solstice, to believe that they had all assembled to dispense justice for a case that had happened in the dead of winter less than a year before. It was only nine months earlier that Jessie had died, but as Carol watched Skrzynski approach the lectern, it must have felt like it was another life, in another place.

Skrzynski began his opening argument with a scathing summary of the events leading up to Jessie's death. He sketched out the diabolic plan the two lovers entered into to cause his death. He portrayed Jessie as an innocent victim, a diabetic caught in a murder plot that two vile human beings had cooked up for their own gratification.

In order to be together, their goal was to poison Jessie with heroin. To do that, Carol Giles violated her husband's trust, blew it to smithereens when she laced his insulin with heroin and injected it causing certain, untimely death.

"As Jessie lay dying, laboring for breath, Carol Giles kissed his forehead. It was the kiss of a Jezebel," Skrzynski told the jury.

The most vulnerable facet of his case was Collier's culpability. Rather than hiding it, Skrzynski seized on it, declaring Collier to be if not the instigator of the plot, then a willing participant. Skrzynski asserted that Collier was enough of a participant to be as guilty as Giles. He told the jury unequivocally that Collier "helped plan and carry out" the murder. As such, he deserved the most severe penalty the law could dish out, life without parole.

Howard Arnkoff, Collier's attorney, countered that his client simply offered advice on poisoning Jessie Giles. Tim Collier never believed, said Arnkoff in his opening statement, that Carol Giles would go through with it. Collier was as surprised as anyone else when she did.

Bottom line: Carol Giles killed Jessie Giles, not Tim Collier.

Listening in the courtroom's front rows, Mike Messina, Kevin Shanlian and Tom Helton had to smile. Arnkoff had just characterized Tim Collier as an innocent bystander. Sitting at the defense table, Collier remained impassive.

When it was his turn to open, John Basch, Carol Giles's attorney, countered that it was Collier who forced Giles into bad circumstances. Tim Collier was the one who convinced Carol Giles to administer the injection to Jessie. If she hadn't, who knew what Tim might have done to her? Sure, she'd given incriminating statements to police, but she'd been aggravated, tired and desperate when she did. As the jury would hear, it hadn't been her idea to kill Jessie.

Bottom line: Tim Collier forced Carol Giles into the plot to kill Jessie Giles.

Sitting near each other at the defense table, the former lovers, the ones locked in a loving, sexual embrace after killing Nancy, barely made eye contact.

As far as Carol was concerned, Tim's talk about staying together had been just that, talk. It was just a con. At the first opportunity, he blamed her for everything.

Tim thought Carol a class-A, number-one rat and bitch. His stoic demeanor belied what he was probably feeling: pure rage that had only been let out when he tortured Nancy to death. And if Carol had kept her mouth shut, they wouldn't be in custody charged with murder.

They'd be free.

June 16, 1998

Skrzynski's case took no time at all.

He had the cops testify to Carol Giles's statements and then offered them into evidence. He had the ME testify as to cause of death. And he introduced Tim Collier's statement to Deputy Peitz that had led them to get a court order to exhume Jessie's body.

The prosecution rested. Time for lunch.

Carol spent much of the break hunkered down in the empty jury box, where she was allowed to stay instead of the holding cell. She looked out at the courtroom, with only a few people seated in the gallery during lunch. Her head swiveled around, looking at the people, and then suddenly her head whipped back so fast, she just about gave herself whiplash.

"Oh my God!"

Sitting there in the front row was Nancy Billiter. Carol continued to stare at the ghost and then her eyes focused on the woman next to "Nancy." That calmed her down.

It was actually Nancy's niece. Susan Garrison's twenty-two-year-old daughter bore an amazing resemblance to her aunt. She was sitting in the front row with her mother.

Behind the scenes, a drama was unfolding.

John Basch had been arguing with Carol Giles, trying to talk her out of testifying. He didn't want her to testify. He didn't want Skrzynski to get a shot at her. But Carol was insistent. She wanted to tell her side of the story. When court reconvened in the afternoon, Basch stood when the judge asked if the defense was ready.

"Call your first witness," said the judge.

"Carol Giles," said Basch.

The courtroom erupted into hushed whispers. The accused murderess got up slowly from her chair and walked across the well of the courtroom.

"Raise your right hand," said the clerk. "Do you swear to tell the truth, the whole truth, and nothing but the truth, so help you God?"

"I do."

"Please be seated."

Messina, Shanlian and Helton thought Carol would violate the oath. Why not? It was time to save her ass. More than likely, she would try to lay the blame for what happened on Tim. At least if she was smart, that's what she would do.

Basch asked her to describe what happened.

"I meant to kill Jessie," Carol said.

Holy shit! thought Helton, just about falling off his seat.

"I know it will establish elements of first-degree murder, but I want to tell my side of the story," said Carol.

It wasn't real. It couldn't be. Only in movies and on TV does a suspect confess to murder on the stand. But here it was, real life, and Carol Giles was about to do exactly that.

Carol's testimony was that she was just fifteen years old when she ran away from home and was taken in by Jessie Giles, a man more than twice her age. He got her pregnant twice before marrying her in 1993.

Carol said she spent much of her marriage nursing her 468-pound husband through severe health problems, including a stroke and a heart attack, despite the abusive way Jessie treated her.

"Why didn't you just divorce him?" Basch asked.

"I had to rule it out," Carol said, "because I was afraid what Jessie might do to me and the children. My kids mean everything to me."

Carol Giles testified that she met Tim Collier at St. Joseph Mercy Hospital, where she worked as a secretary and he as a custodian. They had an affair. Eventually she began to confide in him about the problems in her marriage. Tim responded to her complaints by telling her:

"The best way to get rid of your pain was to get rid of your problem."

"It was Timmy who told me how to kill Jessie and gave me the heroin to mix with his insulin. Tim figured that with Jessie's history of heart problems, his death would look like it was from natural causes."

In a hushed, emotional voice, Carol described in detail how she had killed her husband, Jessie Giles.

She couldn't remember what started the conversation about killing Jessie. What she did remember was it happened in October 1996. What day exactly, she couldn't be sure.

She and Tim started talking about Jessie. They had talked about him before, of course, about how difficult he was and how sick he was. Tim always listened with a compassionate ear. Only this time, Tim seemed to steer the conversation in a different direction.

"Jessie's really sick with a stroke and he just had a bad heart [attack]," Carol said.

She just hated being with him. Tim rationally explained that she didn't have to go on feeling so bad. There was an alternative.

"We're fighting all the time, all the time," Carol lamented.

Tim told her that he could get a gram of heroin and they could mix it with Jessie's insulin. They could make it look just like he had a heart attack, Tim explained. As Tim talked, Carol listened, really listened.

She thought that, well, it felt like the only way out.

"I told him okay."

Sure, she'd be killing her children's father, she reasoned, but was that any better than living with parents who hated each other, who bickered all the time? And was Jessie better off living with his diabetes and his stroke and his heart?

Jessie's time on earth was limited. One of his ailments would get him sooner or later. Maybe it was better to end it now. He'd be out of his misery and so would she.

Carol Giles and Tim Collier talked and plotted a little more until they were ready to act.

September 27, 1997

Carol made sure that the kids were staying at their aunt's house that weekend. She didn't want them around when she killed their father.

That Saturday, Carol went over to Tim's house. He had gotten her the heroin and told her to put it on a spoon and mix it with the insulin. She tried doing it and saw that it was a dark brown color, whereas insulin was crystal clear.

"That's all right. Just, when you give Jessie his insulin shot, don't let him see the color," Tim had advised.

Otherwise, Jessie wouldn't let her do it. He'd

know from the wrong color that something was up. She capped the syringe and took it home. She intended to do it that night, but Jessie had decided he needed to chill out and had gotten a room at a nearby motel. He'd intended to be there for two nights, but they messed up his reservation and he came home Saturday night. By then, it was too late to give him the injection. It would have to wait till the following morning.

Sunday morning, Jessie was in bed, like he always was, watching TV.

I better do it now, while I have the courage to do it, thought Carol. They were home alone; the kids were out, staying with Jessie's sister.

Most of the time, she gave Jessie his injection. The only time he did it himself was if he was gone someplace or if he was by himself. Otherwise, she played the dutiful wife.

It really was a tremendous responsibility, Carol had realized soon after they were married. If just one air bubble got into the solution, if she didn't squeeze all of them out, that bubble would go directly to his heart and he'd throw a coronary.

Air bubble. That was the sort of thing that would show up during an autopsy. She squirted a little of the deadly solution out the top of the needle. She looked at the liquid, cognizant of the heroin coloring the insulin. Both she and Tim knew that heroin would show up during an autopsy toxicology screen. But no one performed an autopsy on a sick fat man with a history of heart disease and stroke who died from a heart attack.

Jessie was watching Sam Donaldson on TV; Sam's toupee looked like it had been sprayed on; he was prattling on about some bullshit. With the syringe held behind her back, Carol approached the bed.

Where to give it? It was an intramuscular injection, meaning it went in the muscle, not the vein. Some diabetics liked it in the stomach, but Jessie hated it there. It was painful.

The other good place was the top of his leg, in his quadriceps, the muscle that ran across the top of the thigh. Usually, for his morning injection—he took one in the morning, one in the afternoon, and one at night—she gave it to him in the leg.

She looked at her watch: 11:00 A.M. Actually, a little late for the injection. Jessie tried to balance it out, to keep his blood sugar level right. But, hey, it had been a busy weekend, what with getting the kids out and going over to Tim's.

"Turn over," she said.

That was it! That was how he wouldn't see it; she'd give him the shot in his ass.

Jessie turned over and Carol pulled his pajama bottom down, exposing buttocks the size of two large hams. She swabbed a little alcohol on his soft skin and plunged the needle in. He didn't wince. He was used to it.

Slowly, Carol pushed the plunger down. It

was like her hand was doing the work and she couldn't control it. She watched the solution flow from the syringe and into her husband's body.

When it was done, she pulled the needle out. Out of habit, she cleaned the injection site again with the swab. It never occurred to her that the last thing she had to worry about now was infection. Nor that he wouldn't be eating, because Carol Giles's first thought after the injection was to go downstairs and begin making breakfast.

Before she could finish cooking the eggs, he called out to her.

"I don't feel good," Jessie said weakly.

She bolted upstairs. He looked really sick.

"I'm so hot," he said.

Carol went into the bathroom and came back with a washcloth to cool him off. As she was applying it, Jessie began to retch. Quickly she brought the trash can over; Jessie threw up into it. He leaned back, apparently okay; then suddenly, another bout of nausea hit, and he moved his massive bulk to the edge of the bed and put his head in the can again.

What was going on? Carol began to feel paranoid. Tim had said it would work within fifteen minutes; he would go into a coma in fifteen minutes. And there was Jessie, thirty minutes after the injection, alive and throwing up!

Jessie kept retching until there was nothing

left to retch. And then he turned and, with the coldest expression she had ever seen, asked:

"What did you give me in my insulin?"

"I didn't give you anything else," Carol answered, frightened he might hit her, even more so that she would cave and blurt out the truth. "Just your insulin, that's all I gave you, just your insulin," she said as convincingly as she could.

By that time, Jessie was catching his breath in short gasps. He tried getting up. He was fighting for his life but didn't know it. Carol didn't know what to do except maybe take him to the hospital. She pulled out some clothes and put them on the bed to dress him.

Yeah, that was it; she'd dress him and take him to the hospital. She had to. Tim was wrong. The stuff wasn't working like he said it would. Jessie had a chance to live if she got there in time.

Fifteen

Carol put Jessie's sweater on him and pulled on his pants. She figured to walk him to the car, but as soon as she got his shoes on, he slid off the bed and onto the floor.

Jessie landed between the dresser and the bed. Carol reached down and put her hands under his arms. She tried picking him up. But that was about as futile as anything she had ever done. Jessie outweighed her by over 300 pounds. She had as much chance of moving him as a boulder.

Jessie said nothing. His eyes closed and his breath came in short, wheezing gasps. Carol didn't know what to do. Her mind raced. She picked up the phone on the nightstand and called Collier.

"Tim, what do I do now?"

Carol looked down at Jessie.

"He's still alive! You said it would take fifteen minutes!"

"You gotta remember he's a big man," Tim reminded her. "Where did you give it to him?"

"I gave him his insulin in the butt so he

wouldn't be able to see the color of the liquid in the needle."

"That's why it's taking so long," Tim answered, sounding like Sherlock Holmes solving a mystery. "Because you gave it to him in his butt, which is farther, you know, farther from the heart than if you had given it to him in his arm. And then there's his fat tissue."

"Yeah, I know, it's thick," she answered, relieved at the explanation for her husband's continued presence on this earth.

"You have to remember," Tim continued, "that he's over four hundred pounds, that it's going to take longer."

"Damn, Tim, it shouldn't take this long," Carol said anxiously.

"Don't panic, don't panic; it will be all right," Tim said soothingly. "The guy that I got the heroin from is right here at my house. Let me talk to him."

Tim's buddy Alphonso Roland had thought, from the cock-and-bull story Tim fed him, that the heroin had been for some guy who lived halfway across the state. Roland had no idea that a man living in a home across town was dying, at that moment, from the heroin he had supplied.

Collier held the receiver in his hand and turned to Roland, who sat across from him. He told Roland what the problem was.

"Okay, Alphonso wants to know what's happening?"

Carol looked down.

"Nothing. Nothing's happening. He's still alive. For crissake—"

"Carol, calm down." Tim interrupted her hysteria. "Alphonso wants to know if his eyes are open or closed?"

Carol looked again.

"Closed," she answered.

Carol heard muffled talking and then Tim was back.

"Yeah, Alphonso says that's normal; he's in the coma now. See, Jessie's a diabetic and Alphonso says that he's in the diabetic coma now. What's that, Alphonso? Hold on, Carol, Alphonso is telling me something."

Carol waited a minute; then Tim was back.

"He says you just have to wait for the heart to get tired. He goes into the diabetic coma and then it's just a matter of his heart stopping. Now, look, one other thing."

Tim wanted her to stay out of the room where Jessie was dying; even though Jessie was in a coma, he could hear everything.

Carol looked down at her husband.

"Jessie, I'm sorry, you'll be all right." Carol bent down and kissed his forehead; showing her continued concern, she left the room.

Downstairs, standing in the garage on the portable phone, she called Tim again. He wanted to know what she was doing. She said she was going to go back and check on him, to see if he was breathing.

"Don't!" Tim hissed. "Every time you go back in the room and he hears a noise, the longer it will take before he dies. When he hears a noise, he will want to live longer, because he will stay with the noise."

Without telling him, Carol defied Tim. She just didn't think it was right that Jessie should have to die alone. Jessie was probably scared already because he didn't know what was happening to him. For her to leave him there like that, it just wasn't right.

Tim didn't care. He didn't want her going back in. But Carol did.

"It'll be all right, Jessie," she said, looking down at the pathetic hulk of a man. "It'll be all right."

She must have waited there a good half hour. At about 12:30 P.M., he stopped making breathing noises. She went out and phoned Tim.

"He's probably dead," she said.

She was going to take his pulse, to make sure.

"Don't touch him! Just get out. Now," Tim warned her.

As she was about to leave, she remembered Jessie had his customers' drug stash right in the house. Taking one of the cellophane bags with a snow-white powder in it, she drove over to Tim's in her Plymouth Sable. Tim was extremely happy to see her.

Alphonso had split, but two of Tim's other friends had come over. He cooked up the powder Carol supplied and made it hard, into a rock. Then he distributed pieces of the rock to everybody and they all began smoking the crack, all except Carol. Tim took a couple of deep hits, savoring the high.

Carol stayed for about an hour and then went back home because she didn't know for sure if Jessie was dead and she didn't know what would happen if somebody came over and just, sort of, dropped in.

"When you get back, call 911," Tim said before she left. "They'll tell you what to do. Tell them you just got home from shoppin'. Tell them that Jessie told you to go shoppin', so you went shoppin'. You came home and you found him on the floor and that's when you called 911."

Carol got back a little after two o'clock. The only change in Jessie's position was that his elbow was now on the floor. She touched him; he was cold. She looked out the window and saw the landlord in the backyard with his son, so she ran out into the backyard and told him to come on; something's wrong with Jessie.

The landlord and his son followed her inside and Carol called 911. The three of them tried to lay Jessie on his back.

"He's so cold," Carol told the operator. "I think he's, you know, I think he's already dead. He's cold."

"Well, just lay him on his back the best you can," the operator repeated for the third, or was it the fourth, time.

Finally they were able to get Jessie, all 468 pounds of him, on his back. The operator told her to start CPR. Carol held his nose, opened his mouth, and almost threw up.

There was something really gross in his throat. She couldn't be sure what it was, maybe some sort of puke.

Carol heard sirens. Squealing brakes. Heavy feet pounding on pavement. The cop seemed to be by her side not more than a few seconds later.

"My name's Officer Barch," he said.

"Carol Giles. That's my husband," she said, and Barch knelt down next to "a large black male lying on his back on the bedroom floor."

Carol stopped the CPR and told the operator that the police were there. A moment later, the paramedics ran in, put their equipment down, tore Jessie's pajama top open, and attached EKG leads. While checking the digital readout, a medic asked Carol the last time she saw him conscious.

Carol told them that the last time she'd seen Jessie alive was eleven o'clock. She had gone out shopping, and when she returned, she had found him unconscious and propped up on one elbow beside the bed.

Bending down, the paramedics checked Jessie's vital signs, quickly noting the lack of blood pressure and heartbeat. His body was extremely cold to the touch.

Carol appeared to be in shock as Officer

Barch led her out to the living room. He pulled out his notebook and pen and prepared to take notes.

"Did your husband have health problems?" Barch asked.

Quickly, Carol filled Barch in on Jessie's poor health history.

"He had been under the care of Dr. Richard Cohen, out of POH."

"When was the last time you saw your husband alive?"

"I left at eleven to go shopping," Carol related, watching Barch carefully to make sure he wrote it all down as she said it. After all, what he was writing was her alibi.

"Jessie told me to go shopping," she continued. "I had errands to do. And Jessie, he planned to watch football," which made sense since it was a Sunday right in the middle of the football season.

Barch looked around and found an open package of crackers on the bed and a package of luncheon meat. It looked like the victim was snacking.

"Anyway, I got home at two o'clock and found him on the floor in a sitting position with his back against the bed. I called 911 and then tried to start CPR."

On further reflection, it seemed to Carol that Jessie seemed like he was going to have a heart attack and he wanted her to leave the house. He wanted to be alone. The implication was he knew the end was near and wanted to die alone, with dignity.

A medic came out of the bedroom. He explained that Jessie had no vitals. They didn't even try the defibrillator to shock his heart. It was clear to the paramedics that Jessie had been dead for quite a while and that any CPR at that point was absolutely useless. The guy looked down at Carol and said sympathetically, "Looks like he's been dead for a while."

The medic called North Oakland Medical Center and relayed Jessie's health information to a doctor on duty, who declared Jessie officially dead.

"Was there anything out of the ordinary in your relationship recently?" Barch asked Carol, who looked him straight in the eye, like Tim advised, and answered with an unequivocal no.

Barch looked around again. There was certainly no evidence to indicate that foul play had occurred. It looked like what it was—a sick man who had succumbed to his illnesses.

Barch gathered up all Jessie's medications to list in his report, then called the medical examiner, which was standard procedure in Michigan whenever a police officer arrived at the scene of a death. It didn't mean an autopsy, of course.

"Nothing found to indicate that a crime was involved. Death appears to be by natural causes," Barch wrote in his report.

Carol watched as the death professionals

shared the information about Jessie's health history and medications. An hour later, the man from the medical examiner's arrived. He was the ME on duty. He did an examination of Jessie's body, still on the floor where he had fallen. He announced that, coupled with what they knew about his medical conditions, Jessie had died from a heart attack.

The state released the body. Carol had to call to have the body picked up. That was a detail she hadn't thought of, not to mention how she was going to break the news to her kids.

She looked through the phone book and found the name of a nearby funeral home, Sparks-Griffin. They said they'd be right by to pick him up.

"The best way to get rid of your pain was to get rid of your problem," Tim had said.

It was dark by the time the guys from the funeral home arrived. They were big, strong men and were able to pick Jessie up and transfer him to a rolling table, the kind with legs that collapsed as soon as you pushed it into an ambulance. Or a hearse.

Since the house was a ranch, they didn't have to worry about steps. If they had, they didn't know what they would have done. They wheeled Jessie out and down the driveway to their black van. They opened the door and lifted him up; the legs collapsed and they pushed him in. With a satisfying *snap*, they closed the door and got into the cab.

Carol pulled the drapes aside and watched from an inside window. The van drove down the street. After a few seconds, it was out of view. And just like that, Jessie Giles's life ended.

Carol picked up the phone and dialed.

"It's done," she said.

Carol was still concerned. What if they did an autopsy and the toxicology screen showed the heroin in his bloodstream?

In that case, all Carol had to do, Tim advised, was tell the cops that Jessie was a drug dealer. He just sampled some of his own merchandise and it was his misfortune to use a little too much. Miles away at his apartment in Pontiac, Tim hung up the phone.

A few days later, Jessie was buried. With him at last in the ground, Carol was now ready to take her relationship with Tim to the next level. Tim moved in—lock, stock and pit bull.

Tim had a pit bull. The day he moved in, he brought the dog over to the house with him. Carol wasn't crazy about having the dog around her kids, not with the reputation of the breed. Tim assured her that the dog was okay, the kids would be fine, and nothing would happen. In fact, he was so certain of that, he decided that Carol could take care of the animal herself.

As soon as he moved in, Carol gave him the keys to Jessie's gold-colored Caddy. Jessie loved that car. It was a status symbol. Now it was Tim's, and Tim decided to use it for a road trip.

On October 1, 1997, just three days after they

killed Jessie, Tim drove the Caddy west along Interstate 80 for California. He was headed for Sacramento, where he'd visit his mom and some friends. He told Carol he'd be home November 3, in time for her birthday, November 4.

As Tim drove west into the setting sunset, Nancy Billiter moved in to comfort her friend and her kids over their loss.

"I just want people to know why I did what I did," Carol said. "When I did it, I looked at it as the only way out," Carol continued, finishing her direct testimony.

"No more questions," said Basch.

Judge Steven Andrews looked at Skrzynski, who got up and began the cross-examination from the lectern.

"Mrs. Giles, how did you feel after your husband died?"

Carol said she was relieved when Jessie died and his death was initially thought to be by "natural causes. I didn't think in doing this that I was going to spend the rest of my life in prison," she said, wiping tears from her eyes.

What else could the prosecutor ask her? She had done his job for him. At the defense table, Tim Collier bowed his head. After that, Basch rested his case.

"I've been a judge for twenty-three years and I've never heard a defendant get on the stand and say, 'I murdered my husband,' " Judge Andrews commented after the juries left the court-room.

"I advised her that if she testified, she would make up the elements of first-degree murder," Basch told reporters afterward. "That's exactly what she did."

Why had she done it? Was it guilt that drove her to make the confession or anger at Tim Collier for suggesting murder in the first place?

Collier had no choice now. He, too, had to take the stand.

June 17, 1998

Tim Collier swore to tell the truth and then promptly testified under oath that he knew nothing of Carol Giles's plan to kill Jessie.

They were not intimate lovers, as she had insisted. No, he was just using her for casual sex. He never gave her any heroin or even suggested she kill her husband. He had no desire and no reason to want to kill Jessie. Why would he?

That was Tim's story. It had been his story right from the time that he'd been arrested and it was still his story. He was sticking to it.

June 18, 1998

During closing arguments, Skrzynski didn't have much to say about Carol Giles's guilt; she had said it all for him and he reminded the jury of that. As for Tim Collier, Skrzynski told the juries that beyond Giles's allegations of abuse, Collier had his own motive for murder.

"The idea was for them to be together, and once Jessie was dead, he lived in Jessie's house with Jessie's wife and drove Jessie's car. Carol Giles told you the truth." He reminded the jury that Tim had told her, "The best way to get rid of the pain was to get rid of your problem."

In his closing, Collier's attorney countered that that statement was just casual advice.

"Tim Collier had no reason to kill Jessie Giles. Carol Giles has admitted to first-degree murder and now she wants to take somebody else with her."

John Basch stated unequivocally during his closing statement, "Carol Giles never had a chance."

Basch reviewed Carol Giles's testimony that she was just fifteen years old when she ran away from home and was taken in by Jessie Giles, a man more than twice her age, who got her pregnant twice before marrying her.

"She worked for him, sold drugs for him, and when the fights became more frequent and more abusive, she tried to leave him," Basch continued. "When she couldn't, she turned to Tim Collier, thinking he was a friend. He turned out to be a monster. She sought comfort from a man who schooled her in murder. He told her to kill her husband and he showed her how to do it. The saddest part of this whole case is that she listened to him."

It was an eloquent defense and he implored the jury to take all this into consideration when considering their verdict.

With closing arguments concluded, the judge charged both juries, explaining the laws, the crimes and what the sentences could be. Then he dismissed them to separate jury rooms to consider their verdicts.

How long can a jury be out considering its verdict? Days, sometimes weeks. But minutes? No one had ever heard of that.

Yet there it was, the bell in the courtroom ringing, signaling the jury had a verdict in Carol Giles's case, and they had only been out a total of twenty minutes. Court quickly reconvened. Carol Giles took her place at the defense table.

"Has the jury reached its verdict?" Judge Andrews asked.

The foreman answered in the affirmative. He handed the verdict to the court clerk, who read it out loud.

"In the matter of the death of Jessie Giles, we the jury find Carol Giles guilty of first-degree murder."

At the defense table, Carol slumped forward and fought back tears. Her jury had taken less time to find her guilty of first-degree murder than she had taken to commit the crime. Handcuffed and manacled, Carol Giles was led out through a side entrance of the courtroom.

That left Tim Collier's jury. Ostensibly, because it was her word against his, it was a more difficult verdict to consider. It was. This time, it only took one hour for the bell to ring in the courtroom.

"Has the jury reached its verdict?" Judge Andrews asked after court was convened and all the principals were in place. Tim stared at the jury.

"We have, Your Honor," said the jury foreman, who handed the verdict to the clerk, who published it.

"In the matter of the death of Jessie Giles, we the jury find the defendant Timothy Orlando Collier guilty of first-degree murder."

Tim looked like he'd swallowed a snake. He must have been wondering, what the heck was the jury thinking? As far as he was concerned, he had done nothing wrong. With a backward glance at the jury, he, too, was led off in chains.

Outside the courtroom, Phyllis Burke and her daughters cried. The three cops shook hands and John Skrzynski allowed himself a brief smile. One down and one more to go.

July 22, 1998

For Nancy Billiter, Judgment Day had come in the basement of the Giles home in West

Bloomfield. It had been a bloody, painful end. Carol Giles and Tim Collier had it easier.

First, Carol was led into court for sentencing, wearing manacles and de rigueur orange prison jumpsuit. She took her seat at the defense table by her lawyer. Court was convened when Judge Andrews ascended the bench.

"Does the defendant have anything to say before I hand down sentence?"

Carol rose. She looked pale and bit her lip.

"I just want to apologize for all the trouble I have caused. I never meant for this to happen."

Judge Andrews looked down at Carol Giles with eyes that showed no pity.

"I've heard from people who claim they are victims, but I haven't heard from the victims in this case—your children. How sad a day when a child has to say, 'My mother murdered my father.' May God have mercy upon your soul."

With that biblical pronouncement, Andrews gave Carol the decidedly unbiblical sentence of life in prison without parole. She was led out. Soon, Tim Collier shuffled in. Nonplussed, Tim took his place at the defense table by his lawyer and looked up at the bench. At that moment, the judge looked huge, like God pronouncing judgment.

"Does the defendant have anything to say before sentence is pronounced?"

Tim Collier rose.

"Yes, Your Honor," he said. "I don't feel justice has been served. I am innocent and wrongly convicted. That's basically it."

He sat down. Judge Andrews paused for a moment, looking at his notes, and then he looked down at Tim Collier.

"The truth is you are a cold-blooded killer; you have no remorse in your body," snapped Judge Andrews, his voice seething with anger. "You planned and helped execute another human being."

Most importantly, he had shown no remorse, maintaining his innocence. But the judge wouldn't buy it. He gave Tim Collier the mandatory sentence of life in prison without parole.

Sixteen

Tim Collier was royally pissed off. How dare that judge convict him of murder when he didn't do anything! And that stupid attorney of his, what kind of defense did he put up?

He had another trial approaching. The last thing he needed was to be convicted of two murder-one charges. Dissatisfied with his representation, he asked the court for a new attorney and the court agreed, appointing J. Herbert Larson as his new counsel. Quickly, though, they had a "personality disagreement."

September 1, 1998

Herbert Larson told Oakland Circuit judge Rudy J. Nichols during a special hearing that he could not represent Tim Collier. He claimed that Collier had threatened him.

Larson said that the threat came during a jailhouse visit when the two differed over "trial philosophy," and Collier told him "there's a bullet on your head, Larson." Collier was apparently making it clear that if Larson didn't get him off at the next trial, there would be hell to pay.

Collier denied ever making such a threat. But the judge decided to err on the side of caution; he agreed to Larson's request and appointed a new lawyer, Mitchell Ribitwer, to take over Collier's defense.

Afterward, Larson wouldn't discuss the threat with reporters except to say, "I think you can say there was a complete and total breakdown in the attorney-client relationship."

Larson said that Collier had wanted him to file motions that would not have been appropriate or in keeping with the law. The threat itself left Larson perplexed, but he wasn't worried.

Asked to comment on his client's defense at the second trial, Ribitwer told the press, "When it went down, he was completely freaked out by it. He didn't know she was going to kill her [Nancy Billiter]. He probably will testify."

John Basch conceded it would be difficult for jurors to look past the horrendous nature of the case.

"The problem we have is her confession," said Basch. "We have to rely on the jury to do its duty to listen to all the evidence before they make up their minds."

"It was a brutal murder and the evidence will show that" was Skrzynski's reply.

Once again, two juries would hear the evidence and decide each case individually; this time, it was before Judge Rudy Nichols.

September 10, 1998

The motive for the murder of Nancy Billiter was still the weakest part of the prosecution's case. What was the reason Giles and Collier had killed her? Prosecutor Skrzynski had a theory.

During his opening statement, Skrzynski told the juries that Carol Giles and Tim Collier killed Nancy Billiter to cover up the first murder of Jessie Giles. Because Nancy had knowledge of what they had done and had to die.

Skrzynski then reviewed the physical and forensic evidence against them, including the battery acid police recovered from Carol Giles's possession that had been injected into Nancy's blood. While he couldn't promise it, he felt that if Carol Giles testified on her behalf once again, he could get the truth out of her. He would have Carol Giles tell the jury why Nancy Billiter had to die.

Defense attorney Basch told the jury of Carol Giles's abusive life and how, despite her statements, it was Tim Collier who killed Nancy Billiter, not Carol Giles. Ribitwer, Collier's latest attorney, claimed the opposite of course: It was Carol Giles who killed Nancy Billiter, not Collier.

* * *

The prosecutor's first witness was medical examiner Dr. L. J. Dragovic.

It took Dragovic almost an hour to describe to the jurors the dozens of injuries Nancy had suffered, including the eleven puncture wounds and injections with battery acid and bleach, her broken ribs, broken nose and, most tellingly, her sodomizing. For while it could not be pinned down to who had violated Nancy Billiter, it was clear that a violation had occurred. The prosecutor would leave it to the jurors to draw his or her own conclusions.

During the ME's testimony, Skrzynski took careful pains to make the jury understand that the injections, though painful, did not kill her. He wanted them to understand what a slow, torturous process her death was.

"What did kill her?" Skrzynski finally asked.

The ME testified that blood from her injuries had flooded her lungs and windpipe.

"She drowned in her own blood. Death was by asphyxiation by inhaling her own blood," Dragovic said.

"Could the process of death been quickened by someone holding a towel to Nancy's mouth, preventing her from coughing up blood from a smashed nose?"

"Yes."

"Are the wounds on her face and head consistent with being beaten by a pistol?"

"Yes."

Dragovic testified to, and showed the jury

graphic pictures of, all the wounds. The jurors'
response was to stare with revulsion at the defendants. Some of Nancy's relatives found the
testimony so sickening, they left the courtroom
in tears.

"Carol was supposed to be her friend. If I
could ask her [Carol] one question, it would
be, 'Why? Why the brutality?'" Phyllis Burke
told the press after the day's testimony.

"She had her life ahead of her," Burke continued. "We're not supposed to bury our children. It's just not right."

September 11, 1998

Kevin Shanlian testified that Billiter's burgundy pullover aided identification because it
bore the name of South Boulevard Station, the
bar where she worked. Fellow employees, who
supplied police with the Walnut Lake address
where Billiter lived with Giles, identified her
picture. Then, when police questioned Giles,
her answers were evasive.

Checking her car trunk revealed blood spots.
A search of the home turned up blood marks
in the basement. The bloody mattress was discovered stashed in the garage.

Mike Messina testified as to Carol Giles's confession and played it, all two hours, for the jury
to hear. Then the prosecution rested and it was
the defense's turn.

* * *

September 14, 1998

Wearing a white T-shirt and black jeans, Carol Giles took the stand in her own defense. She maintained that it was Tim Collier who murdered Nancy Billiter. And to prove it, she finally told publicly why Billiter had to die. As the cops had always suspected, there was a much more plausible reason for her death than a simple burglary.

On October 1, 1997, just three days after they killed Jessie, Tim Collier drove the Caddy west along Interstate 80 for California. He was headed for Sacramento, where he planned to visit his mom and some friends. He told Carol he'd be home November 3, in time for her birthday, November 4.

As Tim drove west into the setting sunset, Nancy Billiter moved in to comfort her friend and her kids over their loss. Everything was going to be fine. Finally. Then Tim Collier got homesick.

Tim never expected that he would miss Carol and the kids so much. But after a day in California, he called every night. He said that he missed her, that all he could think about was her; he wanted to come home.

The wires from Sacramento to West Bloomfield burned up; they talked on the phone for hours. Tim knew he was showing too much weakness for her, but what could he do? He really loved and missed her. Hadn't one of the reasons for killing Jessie been to be with her?

Collier used to tell Giles the story of his past with the gangs in California and his "adventures" with them. He claimed to have killed a lot of people. Carol figured he was trying to scare her, to keep her in line, but she always tried to act nonchalant about it. The last thing she wanted was for him to think she was afraid of him. But she was now, and for good reason.

Tim was a pretty jealous guy. Carol had started seeing him when she was still married. Maybe he figured that if she could cheat on her husband once, she could do it again.

On October 4, 1997, the kids were staying the night with their aunt. Tim was still in California and Carol was home alone. Having nothing to do, Carol tooled on over to South Boulevard Station. Nancy's shift was over at about eleven o'clock and they were going to hang out. Hang out and get drunk—sounded like a good plan to the two best friends. And that's what they did.

After Nancy's shift was over, they hung at the bar, got really wasted, and got into the car to go home afterward. Before Carol could take off, she got a call on her cell phone.

It was Tommy, a male friend of hers from work. They had talked earlier in the day about possibly getting together. Carol explained that she and Nancy were on the way back to her place from the bar and they were drunk. Could he follow them home to make sure they got home in one piece?

In less than ten minutes, Tommy arrived and followed Carol and Nancy home. When they got there, Carol invited him in for a nightcap. They sat around the table in the living room. About midnight, Tim called from his mother's house in Sacramento. That was Nancy's cue.

Nancy closed the bedroom door, but not all the way, hustled Tommy out to his car, and then came back into the living room. Tim had heard the talking, muttering and movement in the background. He wanted to know who was there.

Carol said, "Just me and Nancy. We been to the bar and I'm drunk."

"Carol, who is at the house?" Tim repeated edgily.

"Me and Nancy."

"You are lying. I know you are lying."

She said nothing.

"Who is at the house?" Tim demanded.

"Okay, me, Nancy and Tommy."

Right away, he was upset. There was a conflict of a few months' standing between the two men. Tommy didn't want her to talk to Tim, and Tim didn't want her to talk to Tommy. And she didn't know why that was, just that they didn't like each other.

Tim was more upset that she had lied about Tommy being at the house than the fact that the guy was there. Carol tried to explain, but it didn't work. Tim was pissed. He had just helped kill the woman's husband and now she was lying to him.

Would she watch his back, or would she kill him? Tim asked. Maybe she would have to watch *her* back? The only answer, Tim explained, was to stay together.

"All we have is each other," said Tim.

"And because I lied about who was at my house, you don't know if you can trust me anymore?"

That was it exactly.

During the conversation, Carol Giles's voice got loud, loud enough to be heard in the living room, where Nancy was sitting. And Carol forgot Nancy was there and possibly hearing what was said.

"Tim, you know, *I* killed Jessie. I'm the one that injected him with the insulin."

"But I'm still in trouble 'cause it was something *I* helped you with," Tim answered.

Without him, he knew, there would have been no murder. But she told him that he didn't kill Jessie, she did. She was the one who injected the heroin-laced insulin. Tim countered that he was the "mastermind" of the murder plot.

"The mastermind always gets more time than the person that did it," he told her. They would both go to jail if the cops found out.

"But you didn't do it. I'm the one that injected him, so that actually makes me the one that killed him."

They dropped it at that and continued to talk every few days until the homesickness and separation finally got to Tim. After a few false starts, he left the coast to drive eastward. It took him three days and when he arrived back in Michigan, he strolled in. He hesitated when he saw Nancy.

He gave Carol a hug but continued to look at Nancy strangely. Later, in their bedroom, Tim said that he didn't trust Nancy. During their phone conversation when they talked about killing Jessie, they were loud enough that Nancy could hear them in the next room.

Carol knew where this was going. She vehemently denied that Nancy had heard anything. She claimed she wasn't that loud. There was no way Nancy could have heard. But, Tim explained rationally, on his end he had tried the same method of maintaining privacy, closing the door, and his mom had heard anyway.

"How do you know that?" Carol questioned.

Because his mom had told him so, Tim said.

It was a chilling answer because of what it implied. If his mom had heard their conversation with the door closed, then Nancy must have, too.

"No, c'mon!" said Carol.

"I tell you, Nancy knows!"

"No, she doesn't."

"She does," Tim said with finality.

It was a death sentence.

"Nancy knows that we killed Jessie," Tim stated matter-of-factly. Carol said she didn't, but Tim waved her off. "She was in the house when we had that conversation [on the phone] last month from California where we talked about killing Jessie."

"No, no, my bedroom door was closed and I wasn't that loud. She doesn't know; she doesn't know. I mean, she didn't say anything."

Of course she didn't, Tim reasoned. Who would? She knew and she was keeping her mouth shut.

Carol didn't want to continue arguing about it. Maybe if they stopped fighting, Tim's suspicions would just go away. But they didn't. Nancy heard them talking about killing Jessie. Tim's mom surely wouldn't tell the police, but what about Nancy? How did they know she wouldn't rat?

"So it's okay that your mom knows and she's not gonna tell the police, and Nancy knows and she's not gonna tell the police?"

Tim could vouch for his mom. He couldn't vouch for Nancy.

"We can't leave any witnesses," Tim rationalized. "We have to get rid of Nancy."

Shortly afterward, they visited her father and that's when Carol began talking about killing him because he'd molested her. But did she really want to kill him, or was she just fantasizing?

Tim didn't just talk, or fantasize. He had killed seven people, or so he said. Tim took murder seriously. If he had his way, they'd kill her father and Nancy, making their total kills together three.

Could they really get away with three murders?

They went to Sacramento to vacation. While they were there, the house was burglarized. Nancy said it was Stephanie Johnson; neither one believed she was telling the truth.

Tim was figuring that he should have killed Nancy when he got home from California. But he hesitated—because if he had killed Nancy, without Carol Giles's permission, he would have had to kill her, too. And because he loved her so much, he decided not to do it. He spared both of them. But that was then, and this was now. With the burglary, and their suspicions about Nancy, they needed to get home fast.

The fastest way to get back, of course, was by plane. On short notice, however, the plane fares were outrageous. So were the trains. Their only recourse was the buses. Those fares, at least, were reasonable.

They left Carol Giles's truck with the balky brakes in Sacramento and took the transcontinental bus out of San Francisco. Coming out of the city, they passed through the Feather River Valley, going east. It has some of the most beautiful wooded country Carol had ever seen.

It was soft and tranquil, evergreens reaching as high as the sky, broad vistas of the Feather River flowing through a valley, and glimpses of fishermen casting their lines in for trout. It was a tranquil picture, unlike her mind that was raging.

Their bus hurled through the night. They dozed and then it stopped again in another anonymous bus station. The conversation changed over to talk of killing Carol Giles's dad.

"I have the needles at home," she reminded Tim, "the insulin needles."

"We can use the needles and inject acid into his system," said Tim. Carol thought that was "gross."

The next night, they stopped someplace in Missouri. Around them, people ate sandwiches and drank their coffee. It was a placid, ordinary scene. Carol and Tim sat off to the side in shadows.

"Acid will just eat the organs up," Tim began.

He'd been thinking about it a lot. And then Carol realized he wasn't talking about her father; he was talking about Nancy! He wanted her to suffer.

"Or maybe I could just shoot her," Tim mused.

Carol jumped at this opportunity to put Nancy out of her future misery. She didn't believe any of it anyway.

"Yeah, we can just shoot her quick, quick and over with it."

"No, that would be too easy," Tim replied.

That's when Tim thought of taking her into the basement. All the way home, Tim didn't say another word about it. Carol hoped he'd just forgotten about it.

After three days and nights on buses, they finally got home. When they got in and talked to Nancy, sure enough, Tim didn't make a big deal about the break-in. But upstairs, in private, it was different.

More than ever, Tim was convinced Nancy knew about Jessie's murder. They didn't know whether she'd told anyone about what she overheard, so they needed to get rid of her before things got worse.

Besides, their failure to let him pursue his sexual threesome fantasy still rankled. Tim still thought they were lovers on the sly and nothing Carol could say or do would disabuse him of that notion. Tim reasoned that if the two women were lovers, and Carol moved with him to the Coast, then Nancy, under the spell of jealousy, would turn them in to the police.

Worse, she'd turn *him* in in order to get Carol. She'd tell the cops that he'd done it, leaving Carol all to herself. It was a lesbian fantasy cooked up by a homophobic man.

Tim was fixated on murdering Nancy. Carol, though, figured she could change his mind. *She had to!* She liked Nancy. She was her best friend.

She didn't want to see anything happen to her best friend. It was one thing killing Jessie. There was ample reason and she stood to gain from it. But Nancy . . .

After they had returned home, Tim and Carol left to see if they could find their stolen jewelry in local pawnshops. They had had to pay the taxi driver $20 to take them home from the bus station. That left them with $20 in their pockets. Until she could make some drug deals, Carol planned to pawn her wedding ring while they were out looking. This way they could have some money. Nancy hadn't even bothered to buy any food for the refrigerator.

After searching numerous pawnshops in Huron and Pontiac, they found nothing that even looked like it belonged to them. As for pawning her ring, they only offered her $100. A pawnshop she'd checked with a while back offered her $375.

It was getting cold and Carol remembered a sweater she had in the trunk. She opened the trunk. Staring up at her was her kids' piggy bank.

"What the—"

Tim heard her and came around to look.

"So someone else broke in, huh?" he said sarcastically.

Carol continued to stare. Now she was convinced that Nancy had taken the stuff. She had used the Caddy to transport the rest of the stuff she had stolen and had left the piggy bank in the trunk because she could get nothing for it from her "fence."

They drove home. When they arrived, Tim went to the bathroom while Carol made them sandwiches. She remembered that there were some people who owed her money from Jessie's drug sales. After eating, they went over to collect the money they owed her. The debt collected, Tim said he was driving into Detroit to get the heroin for her dad. Carol gave him the money she just got. Tim dropped her off and drove south to Detroit.

November 13, 1997

Tim woke her up out of a sound sleep. It was 8:30 P.M. He wanted to know if she had any pantyhose. She said she had four new pairs still in packages. Tim ordered her to get them all out and to get the piggy bank from the car trunk.

After she put the kids to bed at ten o'clock, Carol got the hose together, went out to the car, popped the trunk, and took out the piggy bank. Tim took the hose, opened the packages, and went down to the basement to the bed where Nancy liked to lounge and watch TV. She was still at work.

"We'll tie her up," he said.

Methodically, Tim tied the pantyhose to the front and rear of the bed, then tucked the ends under the mattress. Because the pantyhose had a clear color, you'd have to look twice to see it. He told Carol to go out to the garage and get the battery acid.

It was Carol Giles, not Tim Collier, who went out to the garage and came back with the acid that she put on the bookshelf in the basement. It was Carol Giles who came down with Jessie's insulin needles, a pair of yellow gloves and a package of "rubbers."

Seventeen

Listening to the testimony, Helton thought about the condoms. Why the condoms? he wondered. Unless . . .

" 'Cause he said that he was gonna rape Nancy," Carol Giles said. "I can't remember what his exact words were, but he said he was gonna rape Nancy."

If Tim Collier used the condoms to sodomize Nancy when Carol wasn't around, that would explain why his fluids were not found on her body.

Carol continued her testimony.

Tim had told her she had to be "more assertive."

She knew. She knew exactly what was going to happen and what he wanted.

Tim was going to kill Nancy, and Carol was going to be a part of it. Not an observer but a participant. Tim *needed* her to be a part of it. They were in this *together.*

"Okay, I know what I have to do," she told him.

She helped him cover the bed with a plastic sheet. Tim wasn't worried so much about urine as he was about blood. They put the blanket back on the bed and made it up to look neat. Tim put the piggy bank in the corner so it couldn't be seen. Then Tim laid out the plan.

"When Nancy gets home, I will get her high and we'll talk. We'll question her about where the stuff [she burglarized] is. She's gonna tell us where the stuff is."

They went back upstairs; Carol to the kitchen, and Tim to the bedroom. They figured they had all the details taken care of.

Nancy came home about 11:15 P.M. The guy who drove her home decided to be a gentleman and escort her up to the house. If he'd stayed, his chivalry might have cost him his life. As it was, the guy came in with Nancy.

Carol was in the kitchen; Tim was in the bedroom. The guy only stayed a few seconds. He said, "Good night" and quickly strolled down the driveway and got into his car. He started it up and drove away.

Nancy asked Carol if she had any drugs. Carol said no, and that's when Tim walked in. She asked if she could buy some from him.

"Yes," he said affably.

Tim suggested they go downstairs to the basement. That's when Carol noticed Tim had his gun. That hadn't been part of the plan.

They went downstairs and Carol watched Nancy and Tim get stoned. Carol was supposed to start the conversation about the burglary, but she didn't. She didn't want to start the plot going. She hoped Tim would forget about it.

He didn't.

"Nancy," Tim asked her, "where's the safe and stuff at?"

"I don't know," Nancy replied. "I wouldn't, I wouldn't steal, you know. I wouldn't steal from Carol. And bein', you know, that's Jessie's jewelry, that's like stealing from a dead man."

Tim insisted she had taken the stuff.

"What are you talking about, Tim?"

"Carol, what do you think?"

"Nancy, I don't believe you."

Tim took out his gun and pointed it at Nancy.

"Where [is] the safe from the upstairs closet at?" Tim asked.

"Tim, you're scaring me. Stop playing; you're scaring me."

"Do you think I'm playing?"

Carol took the piggy bank off the shelf and confronted Nancy with it. But when Nancy denied having any part in the burglary, Carol whacked her with the bottle/bank and Nancy's cheekbone sank like a crater.

Bleeding, Nancy fell back on the mattress. She was dazed. As her cuts seeped blood and her cheek turned black and blue, she managed to right herself by instinct and crawl back up to the foot of the bed.

After her hands and feet were tied up, Tim slapped her, over and over; hard blows rained down upon her face and head.

"No, don't, please," Nancy pleaded.

As Carol continued to describe the last moments of Nancy's life, she said nothing about questioning Nancy about the overheard conversation. But the cops knew they must have. That was the reason for the method of death: Tim had tortured her with the acid injections to find out if she had told anyone else.

Tim had punched her over and over in the stomach. With each punch, Nancy had groaned in pain. Carol gagged her, and Tim had her start the injections. After the first one, he probably removed the gag to ask who had been told. When Nancy said "no one" and screamed, Carol would have put the gag back in.

A second injection. Carol removed the gag. Nancy was probably breathing heavily and groaning in pain.

"Nancy, did you tell anyone else about Jessie's murder?"

Of course, she would have denied it, because the whole thing was doubtful to begin with. And after her second denial, a third injection happened. At that point, Tim may have been so frustrated by Nancy's lack of cooperation that he attempted the rape, only to be repulsed by her until later. Maybe a few more questions, followed by a few more injections; until Tim would have proclaimed, "She won't answer."

It was then that he would have smothered her; when he knew for certain, when he felt in his gut, that she hadn't told anyone about Jessie's death and they were free and in the clear—if they could just kill her and get rid of the body so it couldn't be tied back to them.

On cross-examination by Collier's attorney, Carol Giles didn't deviate from her story. Just like with Jessie, Tim Collier was the planner. Whatever she did to Nancy, it was what Tim forced her to do, at threat of death.

Then it was Tim Collier's turn to turn the tables, or at least to try.

"I never planned to do it. I never wanted anyone to die," Collier testified, countering Giles's claim.

It was Carol who killed Nancy. He denied hitting her with a gun. Tim told the jurors he just wanted to frighten Nancy, and that was why he helped tie her up.

On closing, Skrzynski said that even if Collier merely watched he was guilty of first-degree murder because he suggested smothering Billiter.

"You couldn't write a more premeditated murder than what was going on in that torture chamber," Skrzynski said.

What could Basch and Ribitwer do? If the jury believed her, Carol Giles's testimony was fatally damaging. They could only counter that the other guy did it.

The closing arguments over, the judge charged the juries and sent them off to deliberate. This time, the verdicts didn't come back in twenty minutes or ninety minutes.

It took two hours. And at the end of that time, both juries pronounced Carol Giles and Tim Collier guilty of first-degree murder in the death of Nancy Billiter. Neither Giles nor Collier looked stunned by the verdicts.

"That's what she gets!" Stacy Billiter, Nancy's twenty-six-year-old daughter, shouted out when Carol Giles's verdict was read.

Stacy clapped loudly. Tears flowed down her face. She had flown in from her Savannah, Georgia, home just to see justice done. As Giles was led out, she glanced back at Stacy with a wistful look in her eyes.

"Not only have I lost my mother, but also my father, sister and brother because she was all of those things to me," said Stacy afterward to the press. "She went out of her way to help friends, like she tried to do for Carol and Tim."

As for Tim Collier's contention that Carol had done it and not him, one juror said afterward that Collier's testimony was "totally unbelievable."

"There's no way in the world Nancy knew about Jessie's murder," said Phyllis Burke. "I don't know if we'll get through this or not. Nancy was a good person. She loved everybody.

That's what I don't understand. She was good to Carol."

October 9, 1998

One more earthly judgment day before the Final Judgment would be rendered. They would have to wait for the latter, Tim and Carol, and they would have a lot of time to think about where they were going.

All of the lead cops were there—Shanlian, Messina and Helton. So was Nancy's family, packed into the courtroom; some members were weeping as they listened throughout the sentencing.

Dressed in jailhouse orange, shackled at hands and feet, Carol Giles and Tim Collier were brought in and took their seats with their lawyers at the defense table. The ex-lovers sat several feet apart and did not exchange so much as a glance or a word.

"Do the defendants have anything to say before I pronounce sentence?" asked Judge Nichols.

This time, Collier declined to say anything. It was probably best; his last speech didn't help. Carol Giles, though, stood.

"I just want to apologize to the family because I know they've been hurt," she said in classic understatement. "I can't explain how all this happened, but no matter how many times I say I'm sorry, this won't change."

Judge Nichols looked down on the convicted double murderers with a cold gleam in his eye.

"You look at these actions, at man's inhumanity to man, and you cannot even fathom it," he began.

Then he sentenced them to life in prison without parole.

"You will spend the rest of your life in prison trying to remember what it's like to be a real human being," he concluded, and banged down his gavel.

Michigan didn't have the death penalty; if the state did, Tim Collier was one person who might benefit from it. At least that's what Tom Helton thought.

Some of Nancy's family had initially wished the state could impose that punishment. After sitting through the trials, they changed their minds.

"With the death penalty, they would not have suffered like my sister suffered," said Karen Clason, Nancy's sister, to one of the press people.

"Does it [life in prison] make it better?" asked Susan Garrison, also speaking to the press. "Nothing will make it better."

Epilogue

Carol Giles and Tim Collier are now serving their time in the Michigan State penal system. They will be there for the rest of their natural lives.

Carol Giles's children continue to live with Maddie Marion, Jessie's sister. No one knows what the long-term effect of their mother's incarceration for their father's death will be.

In March 1999, John Skrzynski got the conviction of a lifetime when he convicted Jack Kevorkian of second-degree murder. The conviction was based upon a celebrated tape Kevorkian had shown on *60 Minutes,* where he administered a lethal injection to Thomas J. Youk.

Mike Messina is still a detective sergeant in the West Bloomfield Township Police Department. He is scheduled to retire in 2002.

Largely on the basis of his fine work in the Billiter/Giles case, Tom Helton has not been rotated back to patrol. He continues to work as a detective on the West Bloomfield Township police force.

Kevin Shanlian is still solving murder cases in Flint. He still has to consciously remember to wear his gun when he goes out in the field.

And the Billiter family? They continue to grieve. They also had some practical problems to consider.

"We were getting bills from the ambulance company that picked Nancy up and took her to the hospital," says Susan Garrison. "It was like we don't need this right now."

Carol Giles and Tim Collier get all of their medical care for free.

A WORD ABOUT SOURCES

The story you have just read is true, but certain names were changed to protect the privacy of those individuals on the periphery of the case.

Interviews, official documents, as well as local news accounts, have all been used in the writing of this book. A few scenes have been presented out of chronological order not for dramatic effect but to simplify the narrative. Likewise, the investigation presented in these pages involved many police officers. For the sake of clarity, the story is presented principally through the eyes of the three lead cops.

The documentation on the investigation of both murders covered in these pages was the most detailed I have ever seen. One can never predict what the appeals courts will do, but it is highly doubtful either defendant will ever be freed on some police or prosecutorial irregularity.

In particular, I want to thank Tom Helton for his tireless cooperation. Mike Messina, Kevin Shanlian and Susan Garrison were also incredibly helpful in providing information about the case and, in particular, their feelings.

Finally I'd like to thank my editor Paul Dinas for his support.

AUTHOR'S NOTE

Throughout the writing of this book, I kept two pictures of Nancy Billiter on my desk.

The first was Nancy, in death, as the police first discovered her. The second was a nursing school photo; Nancy with a bright smile in her nurse's cap. The contrast could not be more startling and more indicative of the life Nancy Billiter lost.

Both the Billiter and the Giles families did not want this book written. They felt that it was dredging up old wounds, which they preferred to keep closed. One family member I spoke with accused me of making money off the dead.

Patiently, but angrily, I explained that if that were true, so were the *Detroit Free Press*, the *Detroit News*, the Associated Press and all the local stations in Detroit that covered the case.

What I do plead guilty to is painting as clear and as bloody a picture as possible of the murders. To do anything else would be to cheat Nancy and Jessie, just as Carol and Tim did.

It is only in the harsh light of investigation,

in an attempt to make sense out of senseless events, that the most barbaric of acts can be finally understood. And accepted.

If in the process I have spoken for the dead, then I feel that I have done my job.

Fred Rosen can be contacted at crimedoesntpay.com

APPENDIX

Note: Carol Giles actually gave three statements to police. Because much of what she said was repetitious, they were edited down in the text.

Yet, despite all she said, the one question that was never answered to anyone's satisfaction was whether or not Nancy Billiter had been sodomized after death. Did Tim Collier perpetrate this crime while Carol Giles watched? Tom Helton felt that the first statement she gave police, in which she said she went upstairs while Tim remained downstairs, was the key to proving this heinous act.

Here, in its entirety, is the first statement Carol Giles gave to police. You decide.

CAROL GILES'S STATEMENT

"Nancy, Tim and I were sitting on the bed in the basement talking about when my house was broke into when Tim and I were in California. Tim and Nancy were smokin' crack (that's why we were in the basement because my kids were upstairs sleep [sic]). Tim kept asking Nancy 'You stole the stuff didn't you? So you could get high?'

"Nancy kept saying, 'I didn't do it, I swear. I wouldn't steal from Carol. She's my friend. When I came home from work Friday, the window in the kitchen was broken. My friend came and borded [sic] it up. I didn't call the police because I didn't know if you had any drugs or guns here. I didn't want them to see anything.'

"Nancy acted as if she was nervous. Tim said 'Your liing [sic]. I can see it in your eyes. Just tell the truth, you'll feel better.'

"I was just sitting in the bed smokin' my cigerrates [sic] and drinking a Pepsi. I didn't say anything. I was just watching Tim and Nancy. Tim said, 'Carol do you believe Nancy is the one who stole the stuff and pawned it for drugs?' I just looked at him. I didn't know what to say. Then I said, 'I believe Nancy that you took the kids piggy bank and I can't prove that you took the VCR and jewelry but I hope you didn't.'

"(Nancy) 'I didn't, I swear I would never do that.'

"I heard a noise like one of the kids might have gotten up. I said. 'I'm going to check on the kids. I'll b [*sic*] right back.'

"I went up stairs [*sic*]. I checked on Lit'l Man (Jesse) [*sic*]. I covered him up and gave him a kiss on the forehead. Then I went and checked on Jesseca. I fixed her covers and kissed her on her cheek. I then went to the bathroom. I turned the T.V. in my room off. I let the cat in the house (at the front door) then I started down stairs. I thought I heard Nancy say, 'stop.' So I walked real slow trying not to make any noise so I could hear what was going on.

"When I got to the bottom of the steps, Tim was tying Nancy's right foot up. It looked like she was tied-up with panty hose or something. Nancy had a white towel or washcloth in her mouth. She had cream color pantyhose tied around her neck and mouth. There was blood on her forehead and nose. Tim had a gun in his hand. He was telling her to 'shut up. Just shut up. Don't say another word or I'll shoot you. Nobody will even know. We're in the basement. Nobody will know.'

"I said, 'Tim, what's going on? Are you doin' this because she stole some jewelry?'

"He pointed the gun at me and said 'shut up.' I shut up. Didn't say another word. I just stood there. I couldn't move. I just kept praying, 'please God, don't let the kids wake up.'

"I watched him punch her in the gut. I don't know how many times. A lot. Nancy only had one leg in her pants. I don't know [sic] they got that way but I didn't ask. I was real scared.

"Nancy was moaning and Tim hit her in the head with the gun. She was quiet for a second then I saw her eyes. They looked like they were saying, 'please help.' I was scared. I didn't know what to do. I looked away from Nancy.

"Tim had the gun. I didn't want him to shoot me. Who would take care of Jesseca and Lit'l Man? I don't know how long I was standing there. It felt like forever. I was feeling dizzy and sick. Tim said, 'Sit down, you'll be alright.' I said I'm going upstairs, I'll be in the living room.'

"I sat in the living room [and put] the T.V. on. I wasn't paying any attention to what was on. I just felt like I needed it on. I smoked 2 cigerattes [sic], one after the other, trying to think what to do. If I called the police, he would know I was on the phone and kill me before they got there. If I just made sure the kids didn't wake up and get out of bed; they'll be alright.

"Tim came upstairs, turned off the T.V. and

all the lights except the light in the backyard and out at the garage. He kept looking out the windows, saying, 'I know she did it. I know she did. Bitch can't lie good.' He sat in front of me and said, 'Everything's going to be alright. I'll take care of you and the kids. Everything's going to be fine.'

"I just looked at him. I didn't know what to say. He still had the gun in his hand. He got up and looked out the windows again, first at the door there at the dining room, kitchen, looked in the breezeway, looked out the living room windows, went and looked in Lit'l Man room, then Jesseca's, bathroom, looked in my room then back to the living room.

"He said, 'They could be out there. They know what we did. They won't come in but they know.'

"I said, 'We didn't do anything. You did.'

"He turned real fast looked at me strange, like someone had took over his body. His eyes didn't look the same. I felt like he was looking thru [*sic*] me. He came over to me. 'We're in this together. The police won't believe I did it. I was never here. We'll take Nancy somewhere. Maybe Detroit. Leave her in Rouge Park or maybe Forest Park in Flint.'

"He looked almost like he enjoyed talking about Nancy being left somewhere. I assumed she was dead when he first came upstairs because he said, 'I know she did it.' I was sitting on the couch, watching him pace the floor back and forth, back and forth. Before I knew it, I had to get the kids ready for school. It's 7:05. I must have fallen asleep. I couldn't believe it was 7:00 already.

"I got the kids up and dressed for school. Tim was in my room while I got the kids ready. Sent them out to the bus at 7:50. Then I went back to the room with Tim. He was smoking (crack) when I came in. He said, 'Sit down.' I sat next to him on the bed. He said, 'I'll take Nancy for a ride. Everything will be alright.' I said, 'Tim, I'm scared.' He said, 'Just remember, look them in the eye and say you don't know anything. If you look them in the eye, they'll never know.'

"I just sat on the bed while he smoked. Time just went . . . on by. He said, 'come on.' We went down stairs [*sic*]. He untied Nancy and wraped [*sic*] the blanket around her. I just stood there. He said 'come and help me.' I couldn't. I just stared at him. He pulled her by the legs and started toward the stairs. Her head hit the door and she didn't scream. I almost cried out. He pulled her up the stairs. He pulled her to the garage. He put her in the trunk of my Sable (I guess because it was parked in the garage).

"Tim acted real nervous. Fidgety. He kept smokin' (crack). 'I'll get rid of all the evidence and the body. They'll never know [he said].' He always talked a lot when he got high. He mostly talked about the passed [*sic*] when he was younger. Talked about the gangs and fighting. Says your [*sic*] not a real man if you do a drive by shooting. Told me of stories of when he was in jail. Says if two people get caught doing a crime or murder they'll use one against the other. That [*sic*] how come he's not in jail now because of all the murders he's done, they could not be connected to him.

"I was scared but I didn't want to show him I was scared because I knew he'd kill me. He always said, 'if you do someone, never leave witnesses. Because without witnesses, the courts don't have anything against you.'

"I carried on the day as if nothing happened. I just blocked it all out. I helped him put the mattress in the attack [*sic*] of the garage so no one would see them before we could get rid of them. Tim and I had a little spat (I told my friend on the phone that I went to California with <u>my friend</u> instead of my <u>boyfriend</u> and Tim was upset). I was scared then. I tried to apologize. I didn't want him to be mad at me. I told him I loved him, I'd do anything for him. I just wasn't thinking. I shouldn't have said it. He told me it hurt his feelings that I didn't love him enough to tell someone he was my boyfriend. He said he would die for me that's how much he loved me.

"I didn't know what to do. He said he excepted [*sic*] my apoligy [*sic*] but if I ever did it again (it being disrespect him,) he didn't know what he'd do. We were talking for about 2-3 hours. I went out into the living room and helped the kids do their homework. It's about 8:30 P.M. Thursday. Tim's in the room and sometimes he would come out and look out the window on the front door. I put the kids to bed at 10:00.

"Tim was talking to his mom on the phone and laying across the bed. I was laying next to him watching T.V. I was dosing [*sic*] off to sleep. He woke me up about 12:00 and said he was going to Flint, he'll be back in a little while. I said 'ok.' He kept asking me why was I looking at him like I was. I said 'like what? It's the only way I know how to look.' He looked at me funny. I smiled at him and kissed him. I didn't want him to know I was scared of him, I sat on my bed, my back to the headboard and the .32 pistol in my reach under the pillow (just in case he come back to do anything). I kept dosin [*sic*] off. I didn't want to sleep. Had to watch the kids. Couldn't let anything happen to them. They're all I got.

"Tim came back about 6:30 am Friday. He packed a bag of clean clothes and said he was gong [*sic*] to Flint. He took the Cadillac. He put Nancys [*sic*] things in the trunk. He said he'll call later. I told him if I didn't answer the phone, I'll be asleep (I hadn't slept very much since Sunday. Hard to sleep on a Greyhound bus). He left about 7:00 am and I woke the kids up about 7:10 and got them ready for school. When they left at 7:55, I layed [*sic*] on my bed. I didn't wake up until the kids got home, at 3:30.

"Lit'l Man (Jesse) was playing outside and Jesseca was waiting for her Aunt to pick her up so they could go to the mall. I looked on the caller I.D. I didn't see any number that looked like it might have been Tim calling. The kids and Stephie came about 3:50. She took Jesseca and Lit'l Man with her to the mall. I think I fell asleep again.

"It was around 5:00 or so when I talked to Tim. He told me to meet him in Pontiac. I went and met him that's when he told me they found Nancys [*sic*] body and he was real scared. He wanted some dope so I was to get it. He'd call me at 7:00 and then we'd go from there.

"He called me and I met him on my way to Rochester. He washed my car and we talked for a few minutes. After I went to Rochester if the kids were going to stay the night with their aunt, then I was going to meet him at his uncles [*sic*] in Flint. If I wasn't coming, I would talk to him later. If they were sleeping the night, then I would come up there. If I wasn't there at 10:30, he would call me at 11:00. If I didn't answer the phone, then he knew I was on my way. If I didn't answer, then I apparently was coming because the kids would be home.

"When I talked to him at the car wash, he told me to go back home and get the battery acid and needles from the basement and bring them to Flint when I came. That's why I was at the house when the police came. I was getting the acid and Hennessy [*sic*] to take with me to Flint."

Carol L. Giles
11/15/97